W9-BCT-731

Ted Schroeder, Jack Kramer, Chet Murphy, Bill Murphy

TENNIS for beginners

Bill Murphy
TENNIS COACH
UNIVERSITY OF MICHIGAN

Chet Murphy
TENNIS COACH
UNIVERSITY OF MINNESOTA

The Ronald Press Company · New York

Library of Congress Catalog Card Number: 58-11240
PRINTED IN THE UNITED STATES OF AMERICA

Foreword

by

Jack Kramer

During recent years I have carefully watched great numbers of young boys and girls play tennis. During my work as coach of the United States Junior Davis Cup squad, and while watching many Junior tournaments throughout the country, I was greatly impressed by the high caliber of play shown by some of these youngsters. As encouraging as the number of good young players is, I wondered why there weren't even more of them, for tennis actually is a relatively easy game to learn if one starts out right to learn it.

The answer apparently lies in the fact that most beginners who take up the game do so with no idea, or at best a hazy idea, of how to go about learning the correct method of playing it. The majority of young players cannot afford to take lessons from a skilled coach or instructor, for a competent instructor usually charges well for his work. Those few lucky ones who can afford to take lessons at private clubs or who are fortunate enough to live in a community where there is an abundance of good adult players who generously contribute their time and efforts to developing junior players usually become our top players.

What has been greatly needed in the field of tennis is a simple, easily understood guide which beginning players of average intelligence can use to help them teach themselves the game. I think this book meets that need.

I have known the authors for many years. I have played exhibitions with them and have been assisted by them in conducting tennis clinics and demonstrations. They have a sound grasp of the many details of the game based on years of playing and teaching experience, and, most important, have devised a teaching and learning method that has proved to be highly successful.

To any beginner who wants to learn to play tennis but who does not know how to go about it, the use of this method is highly recommended.

While this book has not been designed particularly from the parent's point of view, it can be used successfully by the parent who wishes to give his child sound, basic tennis instruction. For them, too, I recommend this book.

Jack Kramer

Preface

This is a book on how to learn to play tennis. It is prepared especially for beginners who would like to learn to play this wonderful game but who know absolutely nothing or very little about it.

Here is presented a new method of learning to play that is different from any other method of which we know. Our method, which we call the Buddy System, is based on the following idea: two people starting out together to learn to play tennis can help each other to learn quickly not only by practicing together but by actually coaching each other, even though both players are beginners. We admit that this sounds like a big order—beginning player and coach at the same time—but we know it can be done, because we learned to play in that manner ourselves. More recently, by teaching countless numbers of beginning players how to use this method, we have helped them teach each other to play. We have encouraged them to work in pairs to coach each other, and we have seen their games improve to the point where they looked like expertly coached players. And they were expertly coached, too, by their Buddies who used our method, but who, only a few months before, had actually been beginning players.

We don't mean to say that our Buddy System, in which you are taught by a beginner, is the quickest and easiest way to learn to play tennis. No method of learning any sport, whether it be baseball, golf, swimming, or tennis, is as good as taking lessons from an experienced teacher or professional. But where competent instruction is not available, the Buddy System can be used as a satisfactory substitute by beginners who want to learn the correct way to execute the various strokes. Also, because our system includes practice procedures and a carefully planned practice schedule, it can be used to supplement the instruction of the professional.

We wish to thank Eck Stanger, of the *Ann Arbor News*, for providing us with most of the photographs which appear in this book. We are also grateful to John Griffith, publisher of the *Athletic Journal*, for permitting us to use the excellent sequence photographs of Vic Seixas and Tony Trabert; and to Bob McIntyre, Colorado Springs, Colorado, for the frontispiece photograph.

We dedicate this book to Bill Parkhill, our high school coach, who spent many hours teaching us the finer points of the game.

Bill Murphy
Chet Murphy

Contents

How the Buddy System Works

In order to learn to play tennis, you must have a partner with whom you can practice and play. In our system that partner will also be your coach. With the aid of this book, you and he can learn together, progressing step by step in a simple, easy manner and helping each other along the way. Our first suggestion is to find a partner—someone your own age or close to it—with whom you think you would enjoy working and playing. Tell him or her about this book and our plan of teaching you how to work together to help each other learn to play tennis. Tell him how we will suggest practice games and drills that will be fun for you both to work on so that you will quickly be able to hit the ball back and forth across the net with what is generally considered to be good tennis form. Talk him into being your Buddy—your partner and coach—because that's what he will be in our Buddy System.

In our system neither player need be an expert player. In fact, we would rather have two beginners working as Buddies, or one player only slightly advanced from the beginner's level. Our system will point out a few things to look for in a tennis swing of which a good player is often unaware. Anyone can follow the simple directions we will set down to teach you to analyze your Buddy's swing, and to help him to make whatever corrections you suggest to him. You can help him to develop his tennis strokes, and he, in turn, can do the same for you.

With coaching and practice in this manner, you are both sure to improve your games. We know you will want to practice because from time to time we will suggest practice games and contests for you to engage in which will be fun, and which will take the hard work out of practice. There will be no wild, uncontrolled shots for you to chase all over the court. By limiting your practice to beginning steps and levels, you and your Buddy will find it easier to control the ball. When you are good enough to make a good score on some simple tests which we will prescribe for you at the beginning levels, you will be ready to move on to a more difficult level. This procedure will be followed until you and your Buddy are able to keep the ball in play by hitting it back and forth over the net.

We know you will want to stay with this system once you have started it because it is fun, even in the early stages. The confidence you acquire when you score well on a test on one level will encourage you to practice hard toward the next level, because you will feel that this next level is nearly within your reach and is not too difficult. Our system lets you know just where you stand and just what you should be practicing to improve your play. You see your progress very clearly as you pass the tests and as you advance from one level to another.

This book, then, will show you and your Buddy how to coach each other; it will point out a few simple things to look for in each other's swing so that you may help one another to develop good form; it will show you how to proceed together step by step through simple drills, to the point where both of you can rally the ball back and forth over the net. When you can do this, you will be well on your way toward developing a good, sound tennis game, a game that will provide you with countless hours of fun and enjoyment for most of your life.

1

What the Game Is All About

Before you actually go out on a tennis court and start practicing how to stroke the ball, you should know something about the game. The idea in tennis is this: In singles (where one player plays against another player), the players stand on opposite sides of a net, which is strung across a court, and, with gut or nylon strung rackets, hit a ball back and forth over the net until one player hits the ball into the net or outside the court, or fails to hit the ball before it bounces twice. His opponent then wins a *point*. After he has won a certain number of points, he has won a *game*. When he wins a certain number of games he has won a *set*, and when he wins a certain number of sets he has won the *match*.

In doubles (two players on a team opposing another team of two players), the idea is essentially the same. The teams stand on opposite sides of the net and play pretty much as they do in singles. However, the court, for doubles, is made a little wider than in singles by the addition of "alleys."

The tennis court

To get an idea of what a tennis court is like, look at the diagram below (Fig. 1). You don't need to know the dimensions of the court or the height of the net (we have asked many champion players what the dimensions of a court are and you would be surprised how few of them can give the correct answers!). Try to learn the names of the lines and the areas of the court, however. You will need to know them to follow our instructions throughout the book.

THE RULES OF THE GAME

There are a number of rules and regulations of the game, all contained in the official rule book of tennis, but you, as a beginning player, need not know all of them. In order to get the most fun possible out of the game, there are *certain* rules you should learn. We have summarized and simplified these for you. Together with the rules of scoring, they will give you the answers to many questions which sometimes bother beginning players.

You will find the rules simply stated and easy to understand. We suggest you read them through several times, referring to the diagram of the court as you do, so that you will get a clear idea of what you can and cannot do as you play the game.

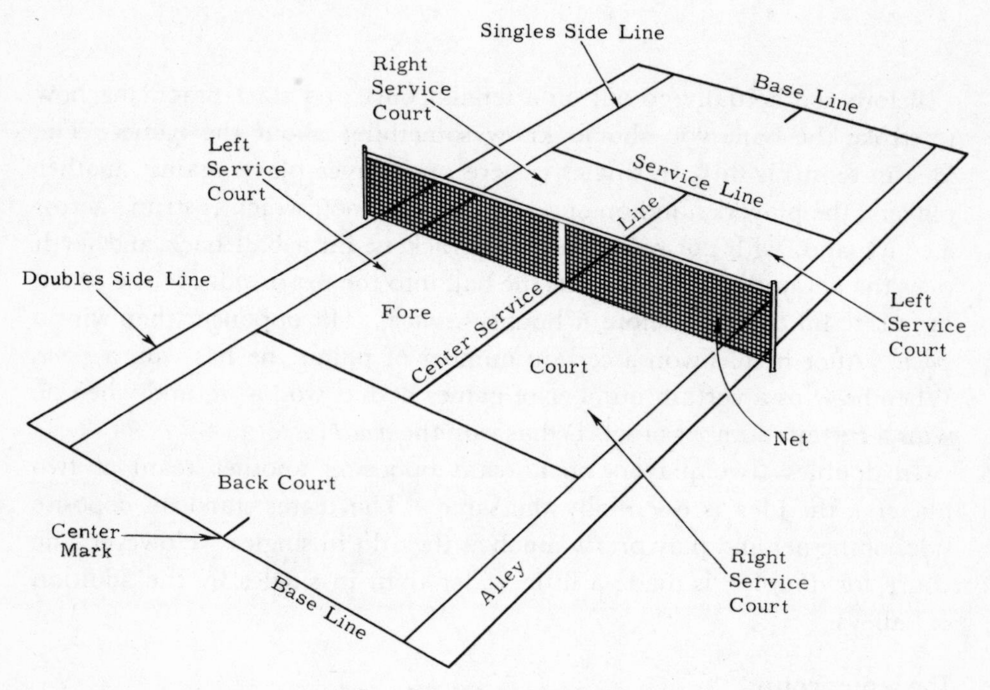

Fig. 1. The tennis court.

Starting play. In starting play in tennis, one player stands behind the base line on his side of the net between the center mark and the right side line and serves the ball to his opponent. In serving, he tosses the ball into the air over his head and hits it so that it crosses over the net and lands in the service court diagonally opposite him to his left.

The receiver of the serve must let the ball bounce and then must hit it back over the net and into the court bounded by the side lines and the base line. Play continues, then, with the ball being hit either before it bounces (this is called a *volley*), or on the first bounce (this is called a *ground stroke*), back and forth over the net until one player misses. That, briefly, is the idea of the game.

Server and receiver. The players stand on opposite sides of the net. The player who first delivers the ball to begin play is called the *server* and the other the *receiver*. The server serves an entire game, after which he becomes the receiver for a full game. Players then take turns serving a game and receiving a game for the remainder of the match.

Spinning for serve. The matter of which player serves first, and from which side of the net, is determined by a "toss" of the racket (Fig. 2). One player spins his racket rapidly and lets it fall to the ground. While the racket is spinning, the other player calls "rough" or "smooth," referring to the manner in which the trimming cord at the top and bottom of the racket face is wound around the gut strings of the racket.

Fig. 2. Spinning for serve.

The player who "wins the toss" has his choice of receiving or serving, *or* the choice of side. He cannot choose both. If he chooses to serve, then his opponent has his choice of side. If the winner of the toss chooses a side, then his opponent has his choice of serving or receiving.

Delivery of the serve. The server stands behind the base line and between the center mark and the right side line. He then tosses the ball into the air in any direction and, before the ball hits the ground, strikes it with his racket. He cannot (1) jump off the ground while serving, (2) step on or across the base line until after the ball is struck, or (3) walk or run into the act of serving. In delivering the serve, the server plays the first point from the right of the center mark and serves the ball diagonally across the court to his left into his opponent's right service court (Fig. 3).

He serves the next point from the left of the center mark into his opponent's left service court (Fig. 4) and then stands alternately behind the right and left courts until the game is finished.

For each point the server is given two chances to make a good serve. A serve that is not good is called a *fault*, and if the first serve is a fault, the server is given another chance to make a good serve. If the second serve

Fig. 3. Serving from the right court.

is not good, he has served a *double fault* and he loses the point. It is a fault if the server swings at the ball and misses it, but if he tosses the ball, changes his mind, and catches it instead of swinging at it, it is not a fault. If the served ball touches the top of the net and lands within the proper service court, or on a line bounding the service court (line balls are good), it is called a *let* and does not count. It must then be played over. There is no limit to the number of lets that can be served, and the server continues to serve into the same court until he makes a successful serve or serves a double fault.

Receiving the serve. The receiver of the serve stands anywhere he wishes, either in front of, on, or behind the base line, or inside, on, or beyond the side line. He must let the serve bounce before he attempts to return it, but he must play the ball before it bounces twice.

Fig. 4. Serving from the left court.

After the serve. The receiver must play the ball on the first bounce and return it over the net to the area bounded by the net, the side lines, and the base line. His opponent then can play the ball "on the fly" or on the first bounce and must return it over the net into the other court. Play then continues until one of the players fails to return the ball into the proper area or fails to play it before it bounces twice. If the ball strikes the net on or after the service return, and lands in the proper court, it is a good ball and is in play (remember, though, if a served ball strikes the net and lands in the proper court it is a let and must be replayed).

Changing sides during play. In order not to give one player the advantage of having the sun at his back, or of playing with the wind, players change sides after every odd-numbered game (after the first game, after the third game, after the fifth game, and so on).

Reaching over the net. A player cannot reach over the net to hit a ball before it bounces; he must hit the ball on his side of the net, although he can follow through with his racket, letting his racket pass over the net *after* he has hit the ball. A player can reach over the net to hit a ball that has bounced backwards over the net if he does not touch the net with his racket, his clothing, or his body.

Striking the net. If a player, thinking a ball is coming over the net, swings at the ball and hits the net with his racket, hand, shoes, or clothing, he loses the point.

Catching the ball. A ball is considered to be good until it hits the ground or fence outside the lines of the court. If a player catches the ball before it strikes the ground or fence outside the court, he loses the point, whether he is standing inside or outside the lines. The ball must hit the ground before it is out.

Line balls. A ball that strikes any part of the line (outside edge, middle, or inside edge) is considered to be good.

Interference. When a player has been interfered with by a ball rolling into his court from an adjoining court, by moving spectators, by a piece of paper which has been blown on the court, and so on, it is courteous and customary to allow the affected player to decide whether or not the point should be replayed. (Replaying a point is called *a let.*)

Doubles. When playing doubles, players take turns in serving and they serve in order. A player from one team serves the entire first game, and his partner serves the third game. A player from the other team serves the second game, and his partner serves the fourth game. This procedure is followed throughout the set. At the start of a new set a team may change the order of service from that followed in the preceding one.

Just as is done in singles, the server, in doubles, serves the first point from the right of the center mark. He then serves the second point from the left of the center mark, then back to the right, and so on during the entire game. The server may stand anywhere between the center mark and the doubles side line when serving.

The receiving formation of a doubles team may not be changed during a set. If Player A on the receiving team plays the right-hand court for the first point of the match, he must play this position whenever service is made by his opponents during the set. Only at the start of a new set may the receiving formation be changed.

In doubles, the serve must land in the service court, but all shots after the serve can land between the doubles side lines and the base lines.

Scoring in tennis

Tennis has a peculiar scoring system, one that beginning players often find very confusing. You can learn to keep score easily and quickly, however, if you follow the method we suggest below.

Read through the scoring chart contained on page 10. Memorize the terms for the points as indicated on the top half of the chart. That's all you need to know: don't try to memorize the remainder of the material on the page but do read through it several times.

Now, on a smooth surface, such as the sidewalk in front of your home or a smooth stretch of ground in your yard, draw a small tennis court using chalk or crayon to mark the lines. Make the court about two and one-half paces long and one and one-half paces wide. Place a stick across the center of the court to represent the net.

Get your Buddy and, according to the rules of the game as you remember them from having read page 4, play a game of hand tennis using the palm of your hand as the racket to bat a tennis ball or lively sponge ball back and forth over the "net." To serve in hand tennis, merely drop the ball at your feet and, after it bounces, bat it with your hand into the proper service court (in regular tennis, of course, you would toss the ball over your head to serve it). Continue to rally, using either hand to hit the ball until you or your Buddy hits the ball out of the court or into the "net."

Play according to the rules of tennis, using the scoring system as shown on page 10. Place this book alongside the tennis court and refer to the scoring page or rule page whenever some questions about scoring or the rules arise. Play a few games this way. You will be surprised how quickly you learn to keep score and how much fun this hand tennis game will be. Undoubtedly, you will want to continue playing it even after you have learned the rules and scoring.

Once you think you have the rules and scoring pretty well in mind, it is time for a visit to the tennis courts. No, not to play yet, but merely to watch. Try to find some experienced players, sit down, and watch them play a few games. Keep score while they play. Notice where they stand in the court, how they retrieve balls for each other, how they are dressed, and anything else pertinent to the game. Tennis teachers are constantly amazed at how much young players learn about tennis merely from watching good players in action. We caution you, however, to be sure you watch experienced players!

TENNIS SCORING CHART

The game

Points in tennis are called: LOVE, 15, 30, 40, DEUCE, ADVANTAGE, and GAME.

0, or nothing, is called	LOVE
1st point won by a player is called	15
2nd point won by that player is called	30
3rd point won by that player is called	40
4th point won by that player gives him the	GAME

except that:

If each player has won 3 points (40–ALL), the score is DEUCE. Then the next point won by a player gives him ADVANTAGE, but if he loses that point, the score is again DEUCE.

The server's score is always called first:

If the Server Has Won	And the Receiver Has Won	The Score Is
1 pt.	0 pts.	15–love
2 pts.	0 pts.	30–love
3 pts.	0 pts.	40–love
4 pts.	0 pts.	GAME for SERVER
1 pt.	1 pt.	15–all
2 pts.	3 pts.	30–40
3 pts.	3 pts.	DEUCE (40–all)
4 pts.	5 pts.	RECEIVER'S ADVANTAGE
4 pts.	6 pts.	RECEIVER'S GAME

Call the score after every point—loudly and clearly—to be certain there is no misunderstanding about it.

The set

The first player to win six games wins a SET, provided he is at least two games ahead of his opponent (6–2, 6–3, 7–5, 8–6, etc.).

The match

Match generally consists of two out of three sets. The first player who wins two sets wins the match. (Championship matches in big tournaments are usually three out of five sets. Here the first player who wins three sets wins the match.)

2

The Tools of Tennis

Now that you have learned a little about what the idea of the game is and know the basic rules, you are almost ready to begin to play. Before that, of course, you will need some equipment.

Choose the right racket

If you have no racket and cannot afford to buy one, go to your local recreation director or park (or playground) instructor. Very often you can check one out from him to use for a short period of time. Rackets are usually marked "light," "medium," or "heavy," but we recommend that you start with a light-weight one (12½ to 13½ ounces). Grip sizes vary, too, and you should use a small-sized handle (4½ or 4 ⅝ inches). As you get bigger and stronger, of course, you will find yourself liking a medium or heavy racket with a large grip (4¾ or 4 ⅞ inches).

The strings in a racket, while very important to a champion player, should be of little concern to you, a beginning player. Any type of standard tennis string, whether it be gut or nylon, will do nicely while you are learning the fundamentals of the game. Later, when you and your Buddy have become more experienced and start playing in tournaments, you will want a lively, tightly strung racket.

We would like to warn you here about a practice that is all too common and that we have found to be a real handicap to beginning young players. We mean the practice of using your Dad's old racket or that of an older adult friend of yours. It is very likely that such a hand-me-down racket, if it was bought by an adult for his use, will be too heavy and have too big a handle for you to swing properly. We have seen many youngsters in clubs, schools, parks, and playgrounds become discouraged and learn to dislike the game because they tried to learn to play with a heavy, large-handled racket that was made for a strong adult. Unless your Dad's or your friend's old racket is light and has a small handle, don't use it.

Use "heavy" balls

The matter of tennis balls for the beginning player and the tournament player is an important one. It is practically impossible to develop a good, sound tennis stroke if you play with old, light, worn-out tennis balls.

By light balls we mean balls on which the fuzzy wool cover has been worn down to a smooth, thin, skin-like cover. The fuzz on a new or slightly used ball is what keeps the ball from curving or sailing wildly when you hit it—it keeps the ball on its course. So important is this fuzz that in most important local and sectional tournaments, and in all national tournaments, the players use three new balls every seven or nine games. Good players sometimes use as many as two or three dozen balls in a long match.

The heavier balls will give you better feel of the ball on the racket, which is a very important factor in developing a good tennis stroke. We have seen many players who have tried to play with old balls ruin their strokes or ruin their chances of learning good, sound strokes. Old, worn, light balls simply will not go where you hit them, and they will float or sail wildly when you do hit them. To keep a light ball in the court, it is necessary to resort to all forms of spin shots, cuts, slices, or to a "patty-cake" push-type of tennis stroke so often seen by the average park player. Remember, champion players would rather not play at all than play with old worn-out balls. If it is at all possible, get new or fairly new balls to make learning the game much easier for you.

Wear smooth-soled shoes

You don't need expensive shoes to play tennis, but you do need some light-weight, comfortable, well-fitting shoes. Standard tennis shoes are of the low-cut oxford type, made of canvas tops and rubber or crepe soles, and are usually white in color. The soles of these shoes are smooth, without the rough notches sometimes found in basketball and softball shoes. Court regulations usually require smooth-soled shoes because, if you are playing on a clay court, rough, notched soles will tear up the clay or make dents and holes in the surface which will cause the ball to bounce badly. If you plan on doing your playing on a hard cement or asphalt surface court, however, you will find that any type of shoe is allowed, whether it be tennis sneakers, basketball shoes, or regular street shoes. Even here, though, it is wise to wear rubber-soled shoes to prevent slipping when you run about the court.

Tennis clothing

Tennis committees and tennis clubs usually insist that players wear the conventional white clothing. A polo or T-shirt, white shorts, and wool sweat socks are standard garb in most tennis clubs (Fig. 5). Public parks and municipal courts usually have no restrictions on the color or type of clothing worn, but it is wise to wear something that will be comfortable when you begin to perspire and will permit freedom of movement as you run, twist, leap, reach, and turn during the course of your game. A medium-weight sweater or jacket comes in handy after you finish playing. Be sure to put it on while you are cooling off later, to keep from catching a cold or stiffening up.

Types of tennis courts

The dimensions of a tennis court and the height of the net are standardized according to the official rules of the game. There is no official or standardized surface for tennis courts, however, and if you were to visit several different tennis clubs, each located in a different geographical area of our country, you would probably notice a great variety of types of material of which the courts are made. Court surfaces vary considerably, and you can find several kinds of courts within your own locality, too.

In general, there are five basic types of tennis courts: (1) cement, (2) asphalt, (3) clay (dirt), (4) grass, and (5) wood. Each of these surfaces has its own peculiar characteristics, and each causes the ball to react differently from the others.

Cement (or concrete) courts, which are very popular on the West Coast, require practically no maintenance or care other than an occasional sweeping to remove dust from the court. There are "slow" cement courts and "fast" cement courts, depending on whether the court is rough or smooth. On all types of cement, however, the ball tends to take a faster bounce than on the softer dirt courts. A smooth, hard cement surface almost always gives a regular bounce, too, though it is a little hard on your feet. Good, sturdy shoes and heavy socks are a must if you play on concrete courts.

Asphalt courts, while similar to cement courts in many respects, also differ markedly from them. They are usually a trifle softer than cement, so that the ball doesn't generally bounce as high as it does on a harder court. They may be faster than cement, or slower, depending on the type of construction used, but they too, in general, are faster than dirt courts.

Fig. 5. The tennis uniform.

Heavy socks and good shoes must be used to protect your feet on this surface, also.

Clay courts, of which there are many varieties, are found in the East, the South, and the Midwest. They usually require a good deal of upkeep and maintenance because the soft clay scuffs up very easily. Popular among clay courts are the dark-red and dark-green types one often sees at private clubs or at schools and colleges. They are generally made of a mixture of clay and brick or stone-dust and are called by a variety of trade names (among others, Har-Tru, En-Tout-Cas, and Tenico). The red or green color, of course, cuts down the reflection of the sun and decreases the glare from the courts. The courts are constructed in such a manner, too, that they dry quickly, often being playable an hour or so after a heavy rain. However, they tend to get a trifle slippery and dusty when dry, and bumpy and rough after a great deal of play, unless they are watered, brushed, and rolled often. They are the slowest of all the different types of courts.

Common, unmixed clay makes a good surface for a tennis court, and you'll find many courts made of this material. The bounce on these is about the same as on a fast-drying court, although often a little faster. This type of court drys very slowly, and it sometimes takes a day or two for them to be playable after a heavy rain.

You probably won't ever see a grass court unless you visit some of our swank private clubs on the East Coast, although there are a few privately owned grass courts in other sections of our country. Excessively dry or wet weather, as well as overuse of the courts, can play havoc with them. The courts demand constant upkeep and expert attention, making them very expensive to maintain.

The bounce is low and fast—much faster than cement or clay—because the ball tends to skid as it strikes the grass. The courts, when dry, provide excellent footing and, if they are in good condition, are a real joy to use. Most of the major tennis tournaments (the "big leagues" of tennis) are played on grass courts.

Wood, on which the bounce is fast and low, is used for indoor courts. Most of our indoor courts are located in armories or school gyms. Wood is a difficult surface to play on because the bounce is a fast one, but, at the same time, its true bounce and good footing make it a pleasure to use.

Regulations covering the use of courts

Let's assume, now, that you have the equipment needed to play, you are anxious to head for the nearest tennis court, and that you are eager to get on with this new game. Here's some information that might be of help to you in learning the procedure used to obtain a court: Many public parks charge nothing for the use of the tennis courts. In many cases, there is not even an attendant on duty to supervise play. The courts are there and are open—usually from 8 A.M. to dark—for anyone to use. Sometimes you will find a sign, posted on the fence surrounding the court, that lists regulations concerning shoes, length of time you can have a court, hours of play, and so on. Read the sign carefully and then obey the regulations.

In the absence of a sign indicating court regulations, ask one of the players about them. Customs vary in different clubs and at different courts, and not always will you know what to expect. Some courts are reserved for a one-hour period of play by the placing of a racket in the net, adjacent to the net posts. Others have racks on the fence behind the court, and players waiting to play place their rackets in the rack in the order in which they arrive—first come, first served. If there is an attendant on duty in the clubhouse or in a shack on the club grounds, he probably has a reservation book or sheet on which he places the names of waiting players. Again, it's first come, first served, except when you are allowed to make advanced reservations.

If there is a court fee, which is fairly common, the attendant in the shack collects it, and then usually gives you a receipt indicating the court to which you are assigned and the time of play. Court fees run anywhere from 15 to 50 cents per player per hour. If you are playing indoors, the fee is usually much higher because it must be used to help pay for the cost of light and heat. Many outdoor courts are lighted for night play. Again, the fee is higher, for obvious reasons. A practice that is becoming fairly common now is for the night courts to have meters, similar to the ordinary parking meter, on a post adjacent to the court. As a rule, a quarter or 50-cent piece placed in the meter lights the courts for one hour.

Court regulations usually specify that the courts are reserved for adults after 4 P.M. and all day on Sundays. That's really not an unreasonable rule because many adults have no other time to play. They are busy working at all other hours when you are generally free to play. So try to do your tennis playing during the adult's working hours and give them the opportunity to use the courts after work and on Sundays.

3

There's Nothing to the Forehand

By now you are probably anxious to get out on a tennis court and to start stroking a tennis ball. You are curious to see how well you can do and you want to begin having fun. We would like to tell you just a little about tennis strokes before you actually start playing on the court, however.

Most expert tennis players and coaches agree on the "basic fundamentals" of tennis stroking ("stroke" means the manner in which you move the racket when striking the ball). Almost all of them teach their pupils to stroke the ball in the same manner; they teach the same, or very similar grips, for example, and the same stance, the same "wind-up," and so on. Our Buddy System will teach you these fundamentals and in the same manner that most expert tennis professionals would teach them to you.

In addition to agreeing on the fundamentals of stroking, most experts also agree that a beginning player should learn to be a "steady," consistent player before he tries to become a "power hitter." The top-flight players in tennis rely on speed and power when they play, but it is still the steady player who places the ball well and keeps it in play who generally wins out in a tennis match. Mercer Beasley, one of our country's leading tennis coaches, claims that 80 to 90 per cent of the points in tennis are won on errors (balls hit into the net or out of the court) rather than on speed. Jack Kramer, one of the leading tennis players in the world, is famous for his hard-hitting, smashing type of game, yet he told us personally that he considers himself a steady player. He claims that while he hits the ball hard, what he really tries to do is keep it in play. Rather than make errors and *give* points to his opponents, he tries to force his opponents into making good shots to *win* the points. He does this by playing a hard-hitting type of game, but his emphasis is on steadiness and accuracy.

It is true that many tennis players have won tennis tournaments merely by "pushing" the ball back during a match and paying no heed to form or style. Players who rely on merely retrieving the balls are often referred to as "pushers" or "dinkers." Few, if any, of these players, however, have won really "big" tournaments, where only the ability to get

Fig. 6. The forehand groundstroke.

the ball back is not sufficient to win matches. Placement, and then speed, should be added to retrieving ability when the opponents are better players. Dinkers, because of poor form, are generally unable to place the ball well or to hit it with much speed and therefore have seldom developed much beyond a mediocre level of play.

Our first objective, then, is to give you practice in the basic fundamentals of the game, so that we can teach you good tennis form, and to help you to develop the ability to keep the ball in play. Good form

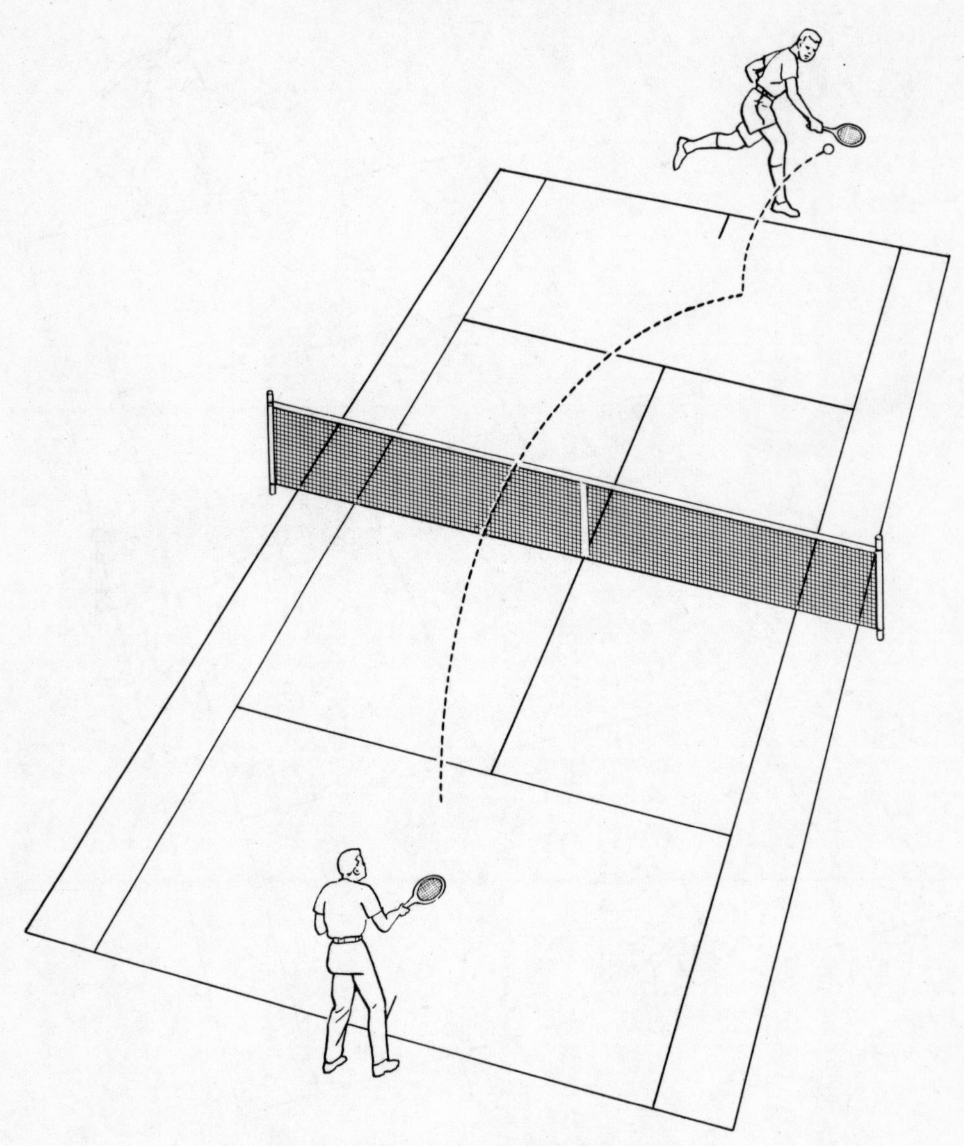

Fig. 7. The backhand groundstroke.

and steadiness must be learned first, after which you add placement and speed to your game.

The important strokes of the game

There are three basic strokes in tennis which you will use about 65 to 70 per cent of the time when you play. They are (1) the forehand groundstroke, or drive; (2) the backhand groundstroke, or drive; and (3) the serve.

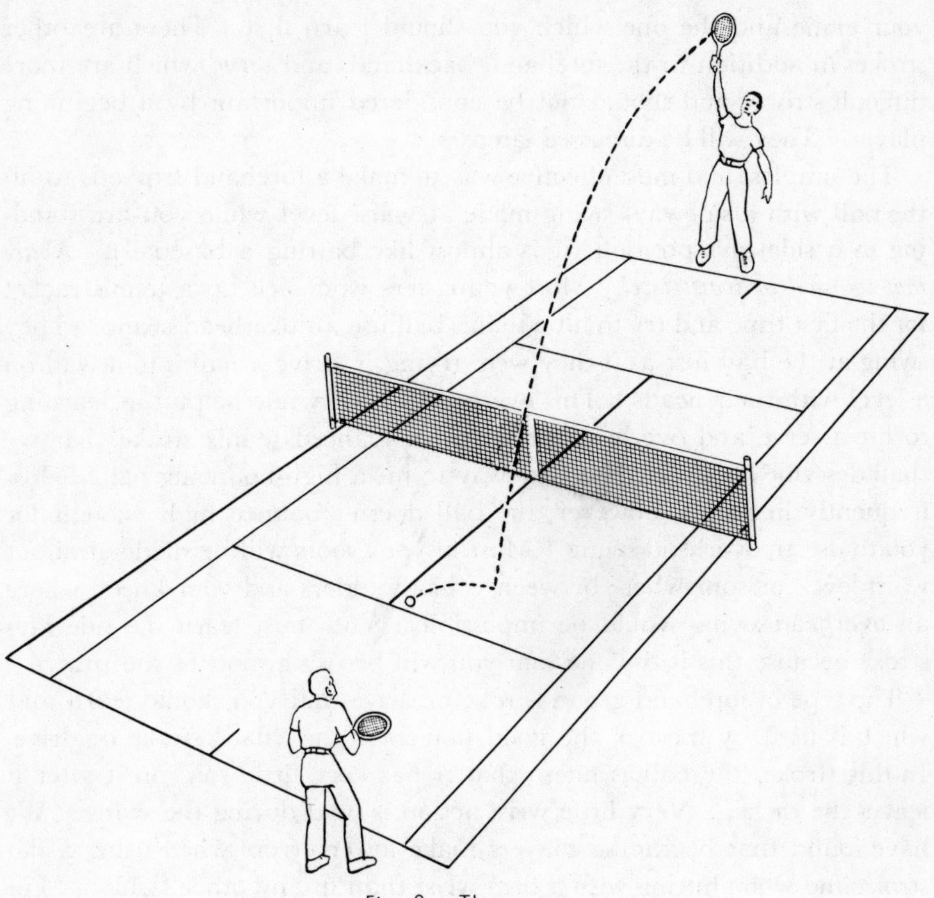

Fig. 8. The serve.

The forehand groundstroke is the stroke used to hit a ball which comes to you on the bounce on the right side of your body when you are facing the net (Fig. 6). The backhand groundstroke is the stroke used to hit a ball which comes to you on the left side of your body (Fig. 7). (If you are left-handed, the backhand stroke is the stroke which you use to hit a ball that comes to you on your right, and the forehand stroke is the stroke which you use to hit the ball that comes to you on your left.) The serve is the stroke used to strike a ball after you have tossed it up into the air over your head (Fig. 8). As you have learned from the chapter on the rules of the game and the idea of the game, the serve is used to start each point in tennis, while the forehand and backhand groundstrokes are used to return the ball after the serve.

Of these three strokes, the forehand is the one which is used most often. It is the basic stroke of the game, the one around which you should build your game and the one which you should learn first. There are other strokes in addition to the forehand, backhand, and serve which are more difficult strokes and should not be considered important by a beginning player. They will be discussed later.

The simplest and most effective way to make a forehand stroke is to hit the ball with a sideways swing made at waist level while you are standing in a sideways position (it is almost like batting a baseball). *Notice that we said at waist level.* Most youngsters who pick up a tennis racket for the first time and try to hit a tennis ball use an overhead swing. They swing at the ball just as if they were trying to drive a nail into a wall on a level with their heads. This overhead swing, while helpful in learning to hit a serve and overhead smash (an advanced tennis stroke that we shall describe later) is the natural way to hit a high-bouncing ball. Most frequently in tennis, however, the ball doesn't bounce high enough for you to use an overhead swing. Most of your shots will be made at about waist level, or somewhere between your shoulders and your knees, where an overhead swing would be impossible. You must learn the sideways stroke because this is the one that you will be using most of the time.

The type of forehand groundstroke or drive that you should learn and which is used by most of the good players is the "flat" stroke or drive. In this stroke, the ball is hit so that it has very little spin on it after it leaves the racket. Very little wrist action is used during the swing. We have found that beginning players make fewer errors when using a flat stroke and when hitting with a firm wrist than in any other fashion. For this reason, and because most expert players and teachers recommend this type of stroke, it is the method which we would like to teach you.

FIVE STEPS IN LEARNING THE FOREHAND

There are five steps in learning the forehand ground stroke, with each step an advancement from, and a little more difficult than, the previous one.

Because you should learn how to swing the racket properly before you actually start to hit a tennis ball, the first step on which you will work is called the *swing*. Our idea at this stage is merely to teach you how to swing the racket properly (no ball is used yet). When hitting a ball, you naturally become concerned about where the ball goes, that is, whether it goes in or out of the court, over or into the net, inside or beyond the side lines, and so forth. If the result of your hit is not what you want it to be, you will make changes in your swing to bring about a better result. Unless you know something about what a *good* swing is, the changes you make might result in a bad swing, or poor form. If you practice this poor-form swing, it will become a habit with you. This habit will be difficult to break away from when you try, later, to do more than merely get the ball back over the net, that is, when you try to add placement and speed to your shot. To learn the proper swing, then, it is best to practice the swing without trying to hit a ball.

Your swing will be built around what we call the Seven Points of Form: the grip, the stance, the point of contact, the backswing, the shift of weight, the body pivot, and the forward swing. These are merely check points which will help you learn to swing the racket properly.

You don't need to memorize these Seven Points. As you practice your swing with your Buddy, with this book alongside you, you will naturally have to refer to the book from time to time, and without even trying, you will soon learn them.

After you have learned to swing the racket properly, you will move on to the second step, which is *hitting a dropped ball.* At this stage, you will use the swing which you practiced at a previous level to hit the ball you drop for yourself.

After some practice in hitting a dropped ball, you will move on to the third step, which is *hitting a tossed ball.* Then you will move to the fourth step, *running to hit a tossed ball*, and finally to the fifth step, *rallying.*

Our plan, then, is to develop first a good forehand drive by teaching you the Seven Points of Form:

1. Grip
2. Stance
3. Point of contact
4. Backswing
5. Shift of weight
6. Body pivot
7. Forward swing

Next, we'll help you use these Seven Points of Form when hitting a ball by working through the five steps mentioned above:

1. The swing
2. Hitting a dropped ball
3. Hitting a tossed ball
4. Running to hit a tossed ball
5. Rallying

Before you actually begin to work on your strokes, we refer you to the practice schedule we have outlined in Chapter 14. This schedule will tell you just what you should be practicing during your first seven visits to the tennis court. Plan to follow the schedule closely during these first seven days. It is the schedule we use when teaching classes and groups, and we have found it helpful in getting beginners properly started in tennis.

Fig. 9. "Shaking hands" with the racket.

Step 1: The forehand swing

On the tennis court at last! We're going to work first on the forehand groundstroke, or drive. We suggest that you and your Buddy go out on a tennis court, taking this book with you, and stand on the base line somewhere near the center mark.

The instructions which follow on the grips, stance, and footwork will apply to a right-handed player. For the left-handed person, the instructions will apply if they are reversed and "right" is substituted for "left."

The grip. To get the proper grip for the forehand, hold the racket with your left hand at the racket throat and place the racket directly in front of your belt buckle with the racket head pointing away from you

Fig. 10. The forehand grip: front view (top) and back view (bottom).

and the handle pointing at your waist (Fig. 9). Now, while still holding it at the throat with the left hand, and at waist level, adjust the position of the racket so that the short strings point straight up and down. Extend your right hand and "shake hands" with the racket handle, being careful to place your palm directly behind the large flat edge of the handle. Be sure your hand is not too low or too high on it.

As you shake hands with the racket, wrap your fingers and your thumb around the handle. We find that a number of beginners like to place their thumbs outward along the top edge of the handle. While this may feel comfortable it results in a loose grip, one that will not stand up when used to return hard-hit balls. Wrap your thumb around the handle, so that it lies between the first and second fingers, and keep it in that position for the entire stroke (Fig. 10).

It might be of help to you, when you are getting the proper grip, to think of batting a ball with the open palm of your hand. Your hand, when holding the racket with the proper grip, should be in the same position it would be in if you were to bat the ball with your palm. Your fingers, however, should be wrapped around the handle.

The backhand grip. Although we won't be working on the backhand stroke until after you have started on the forehand swing, you are probably curious about the backhand grip. It differs from the forehand grip in that your hand is turned one-quarter of a turn to the left, or counterclockwise, so that the knuckle at the base of your first finger is on top of the handle, or nearly so. The fingers are wrapped around the handle, with the index finger spread slightly from the middle finger and the thumb placed diagonally up the back of the handle behind the hitting surface. We'll be more specific about the backhand grip when we start work on the backhand stroke.

The stance. The next important item to learn is the proper stance. The correct stance for hitting a forehand shot in tennis is a sideways one, pretty much like a batting stance in baseball. Place your feet comfortably apart in a position so that a line drawn across your toes or across your shoulders is parallel to the right side line of the court. Now advance your left foot slightly toward the right side line (about 6 inches) (Fig. 11). This is the ideal stance for hitting a forehand groundstroke and should be used whenever possible. Quite often during actual play, variations in this stance will be necessary, but they can be learned quite easily after you have learned the original stance. Even while the ball is in play, you should try to make the stroke from a set stance. Whenever possible, do your running between the shots, not while the stroke is being made.

The point of contact. You have now learned the proper grip and the proper stance. One more thing must be learned before you begin to swing the racket. This is the point-of-contact, or the point at which you want the racket and ball to meet.

Assume the stance we have described in the preceding paragraph and extend your racket arm outward from your body toward the right side line. Don't actually reach or stretch toward the side line, but merely place your arm out comfortably from your body. Hold the racket so that the handle is at waist height, parallel to the ground, and is pointing at the fence which runs along the right side of the court. Advance your arm and racket toward the net and bend your wrist back slightly until the racket handle is parallel to the net and is directly opposite your left

Fig. 11. The stance and the racket-back position for the forehand stroke.

hip. The racket should still be pointing toward the fence along the right side of the court. This position, with the racket directly opposite your left hip, at waist level, is called the point of contact. This is where you want the racket and ball to meet if you are aiming directly over the net, parallel to the side lines. Of course, not always will you hit a ball at this height, at waist level, but if you learn to swing the racket properly at this level you can later easily learn to make whatever adjustments are necessary for lower and higher balls.

The backswing. The simplest way to learn to swing the racket is this: Imagine that you are standing on a huge clock face, with your left foot directly on the center of the clock, and that you are hitting toward 12 o'clock on the face (Fig. 12). Twelve o'clock, then, would be the direction of the net. Three o'clock on the clock face would be our previously mentioned point-of-contact position. Six o'clock, of course, would be directly away from the net toward the backstop or fence behind

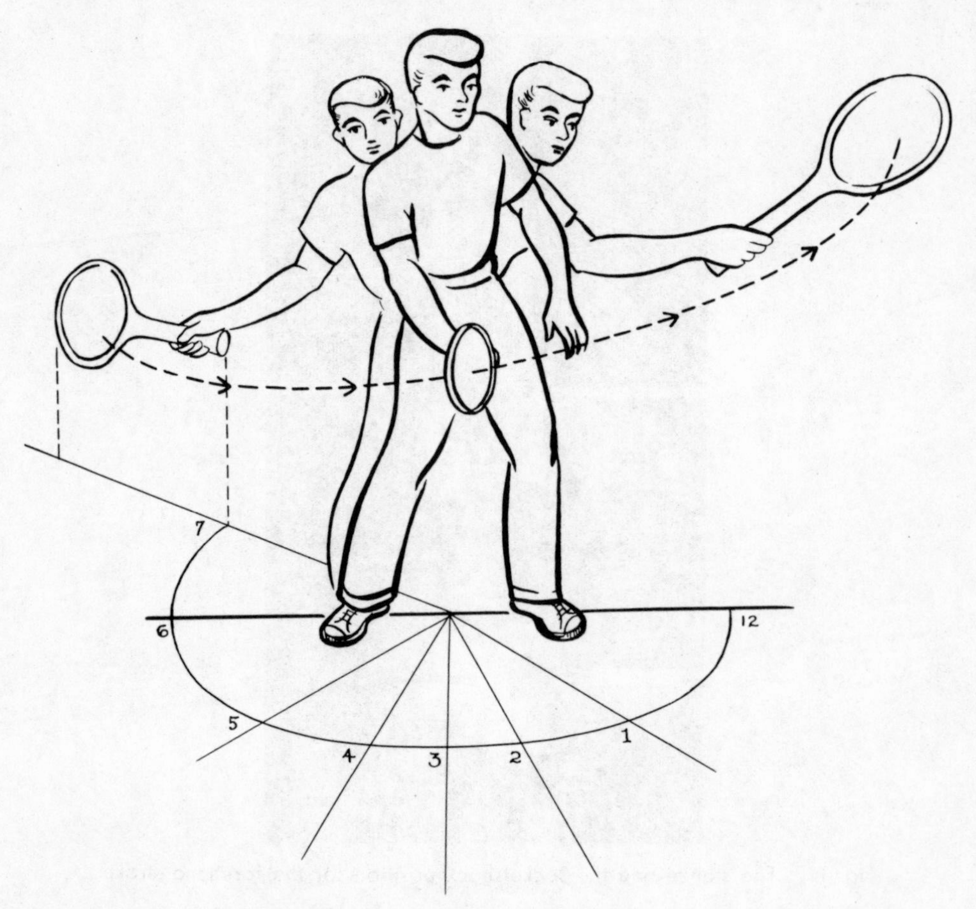

Fig. 12. The forehand swing.

the court. To learn the proper backswing, place the racket first at the point-of-contact position, which is 3 o'clock. Then, making certain that you keep your wrist firm, swing your arm and the racket head backward and slightly upward until the racket is directly over the 7 o'clock position on the imaginary clock, with the racket head about as high as your shoulder. Turn your hips and shoulders a little as you reach backward with the racket until your left shoulder is just slightly closer to the right side line than is the right shoulder. This shoulder turn serves as a windup which will enable you to start a smooth forward swing. Place your weight on your right foot while the racket is over the 7 o'clock position. (See Fig. 11.)

This position, 7 o'clock on the imaginary clock face, is called the *racket-back* position and is the point from which the forward swing should be made when hitting a ball at waist level. If you are left-handed, your racket-back position will be at 5 o'clock on the imaginary clock face.

The shift of weight. The racket is almost ready to be swung forward now, but one more thing must be done first. At the racket-back position your weight has been back on your right foot. Now, take a short step toward the right net post with your left foot and transfer the weight of your body from your right foot to your left foot.

The body pivot. Immediately after you have shifted your weight to the front foot, start pivoting or turning your body both at the waist and at the knees until your right shoulder has moved around and forward, toward the net. When you finish the pivot, your body, from the waist up, should be facing the net.

The forward swing. The forward swing of the racket is combined with the body pivot. As the body pivots, the arm and racket are swung forward toward the net. During the forward swing, the racket head should be smoothly dropped to the level at which you intend to hit the ball (at waist level) then swung through the *point of contact.* From the point of contact on, let the racket head flow smoothly forward and slightly upward to about face level. Guide its course so that it extends toward the net as far as you can comfortably reach.

At this stage of your learning, we suggest that you stop the forward swing of the racket when it points toward the post to which the net is attached, on your left. Stopping at that point will place it at 11 o'clock, which is called the *finish position* (Fig. 13). (There is no need to wrap the racket around your body after you hit, or to swing it up around your left ear as many beginners do. Instead, stop it at the 11 o'clock position, and your Buddy will be able to check for the proper direction of your forward swing.)

Your arm should bring your racket up slightly as it goes forward because an easy stroke is to be learned first, and the swing must be upward in order for the ball to clear the net and land deep in the opposite court. Your wrist should be firm throughout the stroke, and your arm should be extended outward from your body at an angle of about 45 degrees to the ground.

You and your Buddy should go over these seven items, or points of form, very carefully, checking each other to be sure each of you has the correct position for each item. Go through them several times in order, starting with the grip, and working through the stance, point of contact, and so on, checking each other carefully as you do so. When each of you is satisfied that the other has learned these seven points, you are ready to put them all together into the smooth forehand stroke.

Fig. 13. The finish position of the forehand swing.

The complete forehand swing. Grip the racket as previously described. Assume the proper stance and place the racket at the point-of-contact position, directly opposite your left hip. Since an imaginary ball is to be struck at waist level, your hitting arm should be extended from your body in such a way that it slants toward the ground at a 45-degree angle. Your grip on the racket handle, however, will hold the racket in such a manner that the handle will be parallel to the ground. Thus, there will be two distinct lines made by your arm and the racket;

your arm slants toward the ground, and the racket handle is parallel to the ground.

We caution you, when extending your arm, that you don't extend it so fully that it is locked straight. Be careful, too, that you don't lock your elbow against your body. A middle position is best, with your arm neither stiff nor cramped but comfortable.

Your arm should feel comfortable throughout the stroke. Only in the muscles of the forearm and in the grip should there be any tenseness or tightness, and then there should be only that small amount required to hold the racket head level, instead of letting it hang. A "droopy racket," caused by looseness in the grip, is a common fault with beginners.

Now, from this point of contact, take the racket back, keeping your wrist firm just as it was at the point of contact. Continue to move the racket and arm back until the racket is directly over the 7 o'clock position on the imaginary clock face. This is the *racket-back* position. As you take the racket back, be careful to avoid straightening your arm completely. Instead, try to keep that comfortable feeling. You'll find that this can best be done by raising or lifting your arm slightly from the shoulder. This will raise the racket head so that it is about as high as your shoulder. Your weight should be on your right foot with the shoulders in the "wind-up" position described earlier—the left shoulder closer to the side line than the right one. The full forward swing should now be made by shifting the weight, taking a small step with the left foot while pivoting the body, and swinging the arm, all in a coordinated movement. Swing the racket head through the point-of-contact position and on to the finish position, "reaching for the net."

You should spend considerable time practicing the swing with your Buddy who can point out any deviations from the prescribed form that might occur. Each of you should go through the swing time and time again and check each other as you do so. The two fixed points, the *racket-back* and the *finish positions*, should be called to mind frequently when practicing the stroke. Have your Buddy check these positions each time you swing the racket. If these two positions are correct, that is, if the racket starts in the correct position and finishes in the correct position, the in-between movements are likely to be correct also. These two positions represent the farthest back point of the swing and the farthest forward point of the swing.

Here are some things to keep in mind when practicing the swing:

1. Take the racket backward and upward during the backswing. Many beginners let the racket head drop and point at the ground during the backswing.

2. Keep your wrist firm during the swing. Remember you should be working on a steady, easy stroke first, made with a firm wrist. If you have played baseball before you started to learn to play tennis, you may have some difficulty in keeping your wrist from wobbling all over the place as you make the forehand swing. A wobbling, snapping wrist is good in baseball because it adds to the power of the hit. Unlike the objective in baseball, however, which is to hit the ball *out* of the ball park, the idea in tennis is to hit the ball *within* the tennis court. Controlled speed or power is the key in tennis, and the control comes with a firm or barely moving wrist. It is a tennis *stroke*, remember, and not a *slap*.
3. Remember the three check points:
   a. racket-back, at 7 o'clock.
   b. point of contact, at 3 o'clock.
   c. finish position, at 11 o'clock.

Step 2: Hitting a dropped ball

The feeder stroke. When you and your Buddy have learned to swing the racket properly, you are both ready for the next step in the development of your stroke. This step, dropping a ball and hitting it, is an important one because the ability to drop the ball and hit it with some degree of accuracy is something that will be required of you often throughout your tennis career—from your first day on the court to your last. Tennis players, when warming up before actually starting play in a match, drop the ball and hit it to each other in order to give each other practice in their strokes. In this manner they "feed" each other a variety of shots in order to warm up. For this reason, the drop-and-hit swing is sometimes called the *feeder stroke*.

In addition to being used during the warm-up of a match, the feeder stroke is also used to get the balls back to the server after each point. As you know, the server gets two serves for every point, and it is customary for him to hold two or three balls when serving. The balls, therefore, are returned to the server after every point. It is customary, too, for the player returning the balls to the server to return them directly to him in such a manner that it is easy for him to catch the ball. The best way to do this is to use the feeder stroke.

However, the most important use of the feeder stroke for you and your Buddy, who are beginning players, will be to set up the balls for each other so that you can each get practice in hitting the ball. One of you will drop and hit and the other will practice hitting the ball back over the net, either with the forehand or backhand groundstroke, or, later on, with the forehand or backhand volley. Unless each of you can feed well, of course, you will get very little practice in stroking the ball and you can waste a lot of time on the court. The ability to feed accurately and well is a must for all tennis players—beginners, intermediate, and advanced.

Fig. 14. Starting position for the "feeder stroke."

A good method of learning the feeder stroke (drop-and-hit) is to start by hitting the ball against the fence surrounding the court (Fig. 14). You will be working in pairs here, of course. One player hits and his Buddy checks him and coaches him as he hits. Here's the technique for learning the feeder stroke: You (the hitter) should stand about three paces away from the fence. Assume the proper stance for a forehand stroke and the proper grip on the racket and take the racket back to the *racket-back* position. Your Buddy can check these points. If these three items are correct, you should then reach out with your left hand, in which you hold a ball, and point your hand, *with the palm upward*, toward what would be your right net post if you were standing on the base line of a tennis court. You should then let the ball roll forward off the tips of your fingers and drop to the ground. A few practice drops will show you how high you should hold your left hand when dropping. You want the ball to bounce to about waist level, of course, and you will probably find that, if you hold your left hand about shoulder high and drop the ball, the bounce will be just about right for you.

As the ball comes upward, after the bounce, watch it carefully, keeping your eyes focused on it. When it reaches waist level, step toward the ball with your left foot and swing your racket "through the ball" and reach the *finish* position of the stroke. Hold this finish position and have your Buddy check to see if everything is all right. If you have swung through the ball and reached the finish position correctly, the ball has probably gone straight ahead of you against the fence. Practice this level over and over until you have become proficient at it, or until you feel that you have learned to time your swing to the bounce of the ball so that you can hit the ball in the center of the racket each time you swing at it. While you are practicing the swing, however, be sure your Buddy is checking it to see that you swing correctly. You and he can take turns in this drill, of course, so that each of you gets practice in hitting.

After a little practice in hitting against the fence, the hitter should move about 30 feet away from the fence and his Buddy should stand directly against the fence facing the hitter. The hitter can then drop and hit and try to get the ball directly back to his Buddy (Fig. 15).

You can have a little contest at this point by seeing which of you can first hit twenty-five balls back to the catcher. If the catcher can catch or touch the drop-and-hit, the hitter scores one point. Take turns dropping and hitting, with each of you hitting ten balls each time before you change positions; first one of you hit ten balls and then the other. The first one to hit twenty-five balls directly back to the catcher wins the contest. Each hit must be made with good form, as judged by the catcher.

A simple test for this level is to try to hit ten balls in a row back to the catcher. When you can hit nine or ten in a row to your Buddy so that he can catch them without moving his feet, you have made a good score on this test.

Keep a record of the number of consecutive good hits you can make, using the Practice Drill Score Chart provided for you in the back of the book. You should try this test each time you go out on the court for the first nine or ten days. Your score will probably level off or even drop a little after the first few days, but eventually it will begin to rise, and you will soon be able to make ten good shots in a row. The Score Chart will show you how well you are doing at each level, and how you compare with your Buddy.

Fig. 15. "Feeding" to a target.

Step 3: Hitting a tossed ball

After you and your Buddy have learned the proper swing and have spent some time on the feeder stroke, you are both ready for the next step in the development of your stroke: hitting a tossed ball. Accompanying it is a new technique to master, namely, timing your swing to the oncoming ball in order to meet it at the already described *point of contact*, just opposite the left hip. This is not difficult to do after you have learned the swing and if the ball is tossed easily to you. Correct timing becomes increasingly difficult as the speed of the ball to be hit is increased and as you add speed to the swing, so it is best to begin with a slowly tossed ball and a very easy swing.

You and your Buddy will need to work together on the tossed ball drill. It will be helpful here if you can use several tennis balls. Tennis professionals sometimes use as many as three or four dozen when working on similar drills. Of course, you can't get that many balls, but get as many

Fig. 16. Practice method for hitting tossed balls.

as you can. The more balls you have the less time you'll spend chasing those that have gone astray.

Let's say you are going to hit first and your Buddy will toss to you. He should stand at least ten paces from you and place all the balls you have in a box at his feet. He should then toss the ball with a smooth, underhand swing of his arm so that the ball bounces to approximately the same height and distance from the body as previously described. The best way to work on this drill is to have your Buddy stand against the fence on the tennis court. You stand ten paces away from him and facing the fence, so that when he tosses the ball to you, you hit the ball toward the fence.

Before you start hitting the tossed balls, run through a few practice tosses (Fig. 16). You should assume the proper stance and hold your right hand, without the racket, at the point of contact. Your Buddy should then toss a few balls until he is able to bounce the ball up against your hand or very close to it. His toss should land about three paces in front of you. When, after some practice tosses, you have found the correct spot for his tosses to land, mark the spot with a stick or handkerchief; he can then aim for this every time he tosses the ball. When he has learned to make a good toss, you are ready to take your racket in hand and begin hitting the ball.

When hitting the tossed ball, the two fixed points—the racket-back position and the finish positon—should be emphasized in the swing. The racket should be taken back to the 7 o'clock position on the imaginary clock face and be held there in a ready position before the toss is made. The tosser can check your stance, grip, and racket-back position before he tosses the ball. When he thinks you have everything correct and are all set to hit, he should toss the ball so it bounces directly to you at about waist height. When you are hitting the ball, you must judge its speed and swing the racket accordingly, timing your stroke so that the racket meets the ball at the correct point-of-contact position, just opposite your left hip. Stop your swing at the second fixed point, the finish position, without having made any jerky movements or wobbling your wrist. The racket will then be on a level with your head, reaching for your Buddy and pointing just off to his right. Hold that position after every hit, "posing for a picture," and let your Buddy check it. The first few balls you hit will probably not go directly back to the tosser. Many of them will go up over his head, some will go down into the dirt, others will go to the side of him. This will be due to some flaws in your swing, or to the fact that you swung too late or too soon.

If you swing too soon, and meet the ball forward of your left hip, the ball will go to your left; if you swing too late, and meet the ball opposite your belt buckle, the ball will go to your right. You'll have to learn to time the flight of the ball and swing of your racket so that the hit is made just opposite your left hip.

If the balls are being hit over your Buddy's head, you might be swinging upward too much, or you might have the racket head tilted backward as it meets the ball. Swinging downward or tilting the racket head forward will cause the ball to go into the dirt in front of your Buddy.

Your Buddy can check your swing carefully, the two of you can iron out the flaws in your swing, and eventually most of the balls will be going directly back to the tosser.

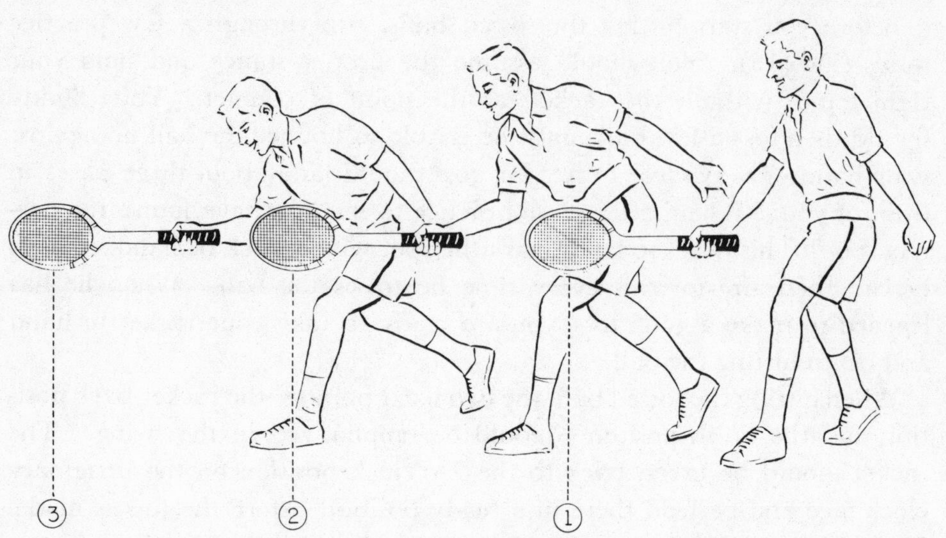

Fig. 17. The distance you step outward with your left foot will vary depending upon the distance of the ball from you at the time of the swing.

Neither you nor your Buddy will be able to toss the ball exactly where you want to each time. Some tosses will be close to the hitter, so that he will have to step forward only, while others will be farther away from him, and he will have to step forward and outward with his left foot in order to reach the ball with his racket. Varying the distance you step with your left foot, in accordance with the distance of the ball from you, will enable you to use the same swing each time; only the distance you step will vary (Fig. 17).

You and your Buddy can take turns in working on this tossed ball drill, each of you hitting ten or fifteen shots before you exchange places. You can have a contest here, too, by again seeing who will be the first to hit twenty-five balls back to the tosser. Take turns hitting ten tossed balls each; each hit directly back to the tosser scores a point for the hitter.

When you are able to hit ten tossed balls in a row directly back to your partner with what he considers to be good form, you have passed the test for this level. Use the Practice Drill Score Chart to keep a record of your scores on this test, marking your score on the chart each time you take the test.

Hitting from a waiting position. Before moving on to the next level, you should learn to turn from a waiting position, in which you are facing the tosser, into the sideways hitting position to stroke the ball.

Fig. 18. The waiting position is much like that of a football player or a baseball player.

The waiting position, in which you are prepared to move quickly in any direction, is very much like that of a halfback in football who is waiting for the ball to be snapped, and like the stance of an infielder in baseball who is waiting for the ball to be hit toward him (Fig. 18). In this position your knees should be slightly bent and your body should be inclined forward slightly. Grip the racket properly with your right hand and hold the racket in front of you, resting its throat lightly in your left hand.

As the ball is tossed, you should move into a hitting position by turning your body sideways while crossing your left foot over your right foot, and pivoting on the sole of your right foot. At the same time, bring your racket back to the racket-back position. As the ball arrives, merely "step into it" with your left foot and swing the racket forward to stroke the ball.

Alternate hitting and tossing with your Buddy until each of you can make the turn and hit ten balls in a row back to the tosser.

Step 4: Running and hitting a tossed ball

As you know, when playing tennis your opponent in most cases tries to hit the ball away from you. He tries to make you run to get you out of position and to make it difficult for you to get the ball back over the net and into the court. You always have to make some sort of movement, either to the side, forward, or backward, to get in the proper position to hit the ball. Running to the ball, of course, involves footwork, which is the use of your feet to get into position to hit the ball. This is our next level: learning to run and hit a tossed ball.

This level is more difficult than the previous one because it involves not only timing the swing of the racket to the flight of the ball but also timing your running speed as you run to the ball. You must learn to time your running so that you arrive at the proper position (where the ball will be) in time to stroke it properly.

Here is the way you should practice this level: Let's assume again that you will hit and your Buddy will toss. You should stand on the base line, midway between the side lines, directly on the center mark of the court. Your Buddy should stand on the right singles side line (your right side line) and ten paces from your base line (toward the net).

You should assume the hitting position, with your knees slightly bent, your feet comfortably spread, and your body in a sideways position with the racket at the racket-back position. Your Buddy, who can check your grip, stance, and racket-back position, tosses the ball when he thinks you have everything correct and are ready to run. He should toss the ball underhanded directly along the side line so that it bounces to your waist level at the junction of the base line and the side line.

As soon as the ball leaves his hand, you should start running along the base line, keeping your racket in the racket-back position. Keep your eyes on the ball. When you get to the side line, stop running, step forward with your left foot, and hit the ball. Hold your finish position and let your Buddy check it.

The footwork involved in running for the ball is very important in tennis. You should spend some time practicing it. As you will notice when you run to hit a ball, not always will your feet end in the proper position, that is, with the left foot forward. Quite often you will have to make some adjustments in your steps as you run toward the ball. These adjustments are made in the following manner: If, as you run toward the ball, you decide that you are going to get too close to it or end up with the wrong foot forward, you should take several small skipping steps (or "half steps") in order for your feet to end in the proper position. These small, skipping half steps are taken at the last moment, if necessary, by advancing the right foot forward to a position even with the left foot and then skipping the left foot forward to its proper position in the stance. These skipping, or dancing, steps are necessary for a player to get into the proper position when running for the ball. If you have watched some good players play, you have probably noticed how they seem to skip or dance around the court. They appear to be very light on their feet and never seem to be running very hard or heavily.

You may find as you practice this drill that you get to the point at which the side line meets the base line before the ball does. All you have to do, then, is wait for the ball, with your racket back. When the ball finally does get to this point, merely step into it and hit it. If you get there too late, you have to hurry a little more the next time you run along the base line. The test for this level is the same as for the previous one: Try to hit ten consecutive balls back to your Buddy so that he can catch the ball without moving his feet. Your scores on this test can be recorded on the Practice Drill Score Chart so that you can see just how well you are doing. Remember, when taking the test, that each hit should be made with proper form. Your Buddy can check your form each time you hit and tell you what you are doing wrong; he can make the necessary suggestions to correct your form, too.

After you and your Buddy have passed this level, you can vary the drill a little bit and make it a little more difficult in the following manner: Your Buddy should stand at the net on the center line of the court. You should stand on the base line directly over the center mark. Your Buddy should then toss the ball various distances away from you off to your right, trying to make you run just a few steps on some occasions and several steps on other occasions. With practice in this manner, you will learn how fast you have to run to get to the ball. This is also excellent practice in footwork, because you will learn when to skip to the ball with half steps and when not to skip.

Another variation is to have the hitter stand in a waiting position, facing the tosser. As the ball is tossed, he must turn sideways, by crossing his left foot over his right foot, and begin his backswing. He must then run to where he thinks the ball will be and take his racket back as he does so.

Hitting a ball that comes directly at you. At this time, too, you could practice turning away from a ball that comes directly at you and then stroking it. When the ball does come directly at you, you can play it on either side—forehand or backhand, whichever you prefer. For the time being, play them on the forehand side, using a forehand stroke, by merely swinging your right foot backward and to the left, toward the left side line, while you pivot on the sole of your left foot. Take your racket back while you turn. When the ball arrives, you merely have to step into it and complete your stroke.

This drill should be practiced for some time by both you and your Buddy because quite often during a match you are forced to play balls that come directly at you.

Hitting high and low balls. When you are able to run and hit ten consecutively tossed balls directly back to the tosser, you should learn to hit balls at various heights before going on to *rallying*, which is the final level. While you are rallying, you cannot depend upon the ball to come back to you at waist level every time, so you must learn to hit balls that bounce higher and lower than your waist.

For a lower bounce than has been used thus far, merely bend your knees until the plane of your swing coincides with the height of the ball and swing through the ball as before. The bending of the knees is the only change in the stroke except on very low shots, those that are just barely off the ground. Your arm should still be back at a 45-degree angle to the ground, and the racket should be parallel to the ground or pointing only slightly at the ground, and it should be directly behind and a little below where the ball is to be hit (Fig. 19). Your knees should be bent throughout the entire stroke. This will be one more item to be checked at the finish of the stroke when hitting a low ball.

When hitting a shoulder-high ball, the racket should be raised to the racket-back position by moving your arm at the shoulder joint only up to a point behind where the ball is to be hit. Everything else is the same, and the swing is made as before into the line of flight.

Fig. 19. Hitting a low forehand.

Step 5: Rallying

The final stage in learning to hit the forehand drive is rallying. The term *rally* in tennis means, simply, to keep the ball in play as long as possible. It refers to any practice drill in which the ball is kept in play, the warm-up period before play actually begins in a match, or to any pro-

Fig. 20. Rallying against a bangboard.

longed exchange during the course of actual play. We'll use the term here to mean practice drills, where you and your Buddy merely try to return the ball to each other, keeping it in play.

You and your Buddy should stand on opposite sides of the net, about 2 feet behind the base line, and midway between the two side lines. One player should start the rally by dropping the ball and hitting it (refer to what you learned in the drop-and-hit drill) so that it crosses the center of the net about 5 or 6 feet above the net top. His partner should then play the ball on the first bounce and try to hit it directly back over the center of the net. Both players should then try to keep the ball in play, moving to it so that they can play it at waist level. You'll find that you will have to move forward or backward in the court, or to the left or to the right, depending upon the length and direction of your Buddy's shot, but try always to return to your original starting position after you make each stroke. Don't go too far forward to play a short shot that your Buddy makes; instead, wait for the very short balls to come back to you and play them on the second bounce, or catch them and start the rally over.

Fig. 21. Trying to "out-steady" each other against a bangboard.

When you are moving around the court to get to the ball or to return to the center of the court, take short, quick steps. Try always, too, to place your body in the proper hitting position (sideways) for stroking the ball. Remember, also, to get the racket back early so that your swing will not have to be hurried.

Don't try to hit the balls too hard—concentrate on steadiness and accuracy, trying only to get the ball back deep to your Buddy. Try to keep the ball in play as long as you can, counting the number of times each of you can hit the ball before one of you hits it out of the court or into the net, or so far on his Buddy's backhand side that he can't play a forehand stroke. We saw two beginners, who had only been playing tennis for one week, each hit the ball fifteen times before one of them missed.

When you and your Buddy can each hit ten balls back in a row without a miss, you have passed the test for this level. Keep a record of how long you can rally without missing by counting the number of times you and your Buddy can each hit the ball before one of you misses.

Rallying against a bangboard. A very good method of improving your timing, judgment, and stroking is to practice rallying against a bangboard. A bangboard is merely a wooden or brick wall against which you hit balls. Most tennis clubs and parks have them adjacent to the tennis courts. Very often the side of a building or the wall of a gymnasium can be used as a substitute (Fig. 20).

To start a rally against a bangboard, stand about ten paces away from it (in a hitting position), drop the ball, and hit it against the wall, using the feeder stroke. As the ball comes back to you, move to the proper position while you take the racket back, and hit it again, trying to keep it in play.

Don't get discouraged if at first you can't control the ball. With a little practice you'll be surprised how quickly you improve. We warn you not to be so anxious to get the ball back to the wall that you forget about stroking it properly.

Many good players have spent much time in practice against a bangboard to improve their games. Mrs. Jean Hoxie, one of the country's leading developers of junior players, has her pupils spend many hours in bangboard practice in order to improve their timing, judgment, and footwork practice. By applying simple handball rules, she has her pupils try to "out-steady" each other against the bangboard. Try it—it's loads of fun and good practice, too (Fig. 21).

In addition, aiming at targets marked on the bangboard will help you develop your stroke. It is an easy matter to mark a target, such as a square or circle; about two racket lengths above the ground is the right height for these targets. We suggest you practice hitting the targets and keep score of the number of successful hits. You will notice the Practice Drill Score Chart has a column for recording your scores.

4

Don't Be Afraid of Backhands

The backhand groundstroke is the second most important stroke of the game. Most tennis players have weaker backhand strokes than they have forehand strokes. Their opponents, if they are aware of the weak backhand, will play most of their shots there and force them to hit many backhands.

Most beginning players dread even the thought of hitting a backhand. They feel that it is not a natural stroke and one that is difficult to learn, although it is no more so than the forehand. Indeed, many of our ranking players have a better backhand, and many would prefer to hit a backhand rather than a forehand. Jack Kramer and Don Budge, two of the greatest players in the history of tennis, scored many more points during their tennis careers by hitting aggressive backhand shots than they did forehand shots.

As in the forehand, the simplest and most effective method of making a backhand stroke is to hit the ball while you are in a sideways stance. Here, however, your sideways position is reversed from that of the forehand. Instead of facing the right side line, you should, if you are a right-handed player, face the left side line as you stroke the ball (Fig. 22). As in the forehand stroke, the type backhand groundstroke or drive you should learn, and which is used the most by good players, is the flat stroke or drive. Here, again, the ball is hit so that it has very little spin on it after it leaves your racket. Very little wrist action is used during the swing.

FOUR STEPS IN LEARNING THE BACKHAND GROUNDSTROKE

The backhand groundstroke can be learned just as the forehand groundstroke was learned: by progressing or working through steps. Each step is an advancement from and a little more difficult than the previous one. There is one exception, however, when working on the backhand groundstroke: the dropped-ball step can be eliminated be-

Fig. 22. The backhand drive.

Tony Trabert, former U. S. Davis Cup star and now a professional, is shown executing a low backhand drive. He turns his body sideways to the net and completes his backswing in one rhythmic movement. As he begins the stroke from the top of the backswing,

cause it is difficult for a player to drop the ball for himself and hit a backhand. Work, then, would progress (in much the same manner as it did on the forehand) through the following steps: the swing, hitting a tossed ball, running to hit a tossed ball, and rallying.

The backhand swing will be built around the Seven Points of Form: (1) grip, (2) stance, (3) point of contact, (4) backswing, (5) shift of weight, (6) body pivot, and (7) forward swing.

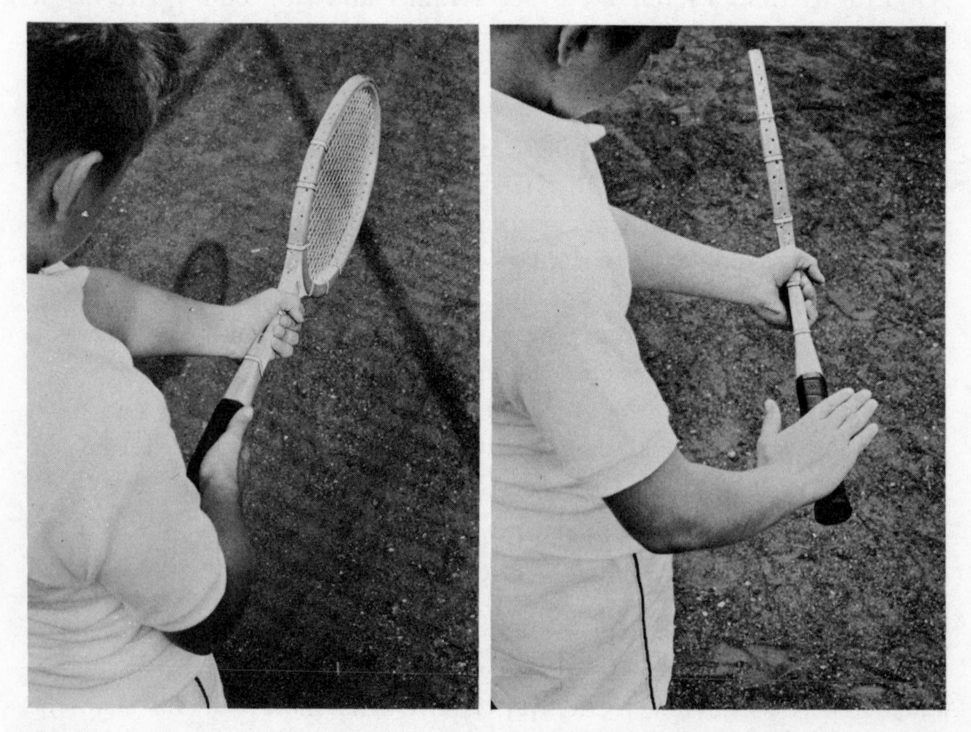

Fig. 23. From the forehand position (left) your hand should be turned $\frac{1}{4}$ of a turn to your left to get the proper backhand grip position (right).

(photo courtesy of the *Athletic Journal*)

he shifts his weight from the left foot to the right foot, timing his forward swing so that his racket meets the ball at a point several inches in front of his right knee. Note that his knees are well bent for this low shot.

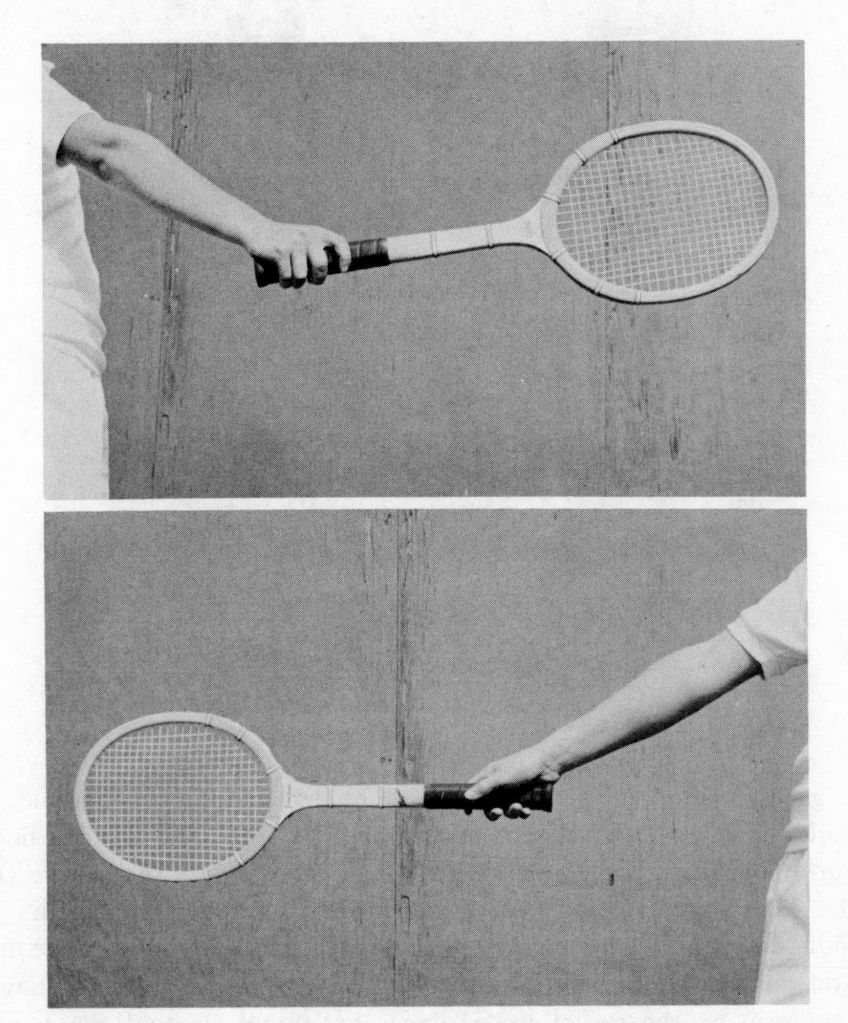

Fig. 24. The backhand grip showing at the top the front view and at the bottom the back view.

Step 1: The swing

The grip. The backhand grip differs from the forehand grip in that your hand is turned counterclockwise, one-quarter of a turn to the left from the forehand grip, so that the first knuckle of your hand is directly on top of the handle if the racket face is in a perpendicular position to

Fig. 25. The point of contact for the backhand stroke.

the ground (Fig. 23). Your fingers should be wrapped around the handle, with the index finger spread slightly from the middle finger. Your thumb should be placed diagonally up the back of the handle (Fig. 24). Many good players place their thumb completely around the handle and suggest this method as a proper backhand grip. We have found through experience, however, that the beginner seems to have a firmer grip on the racket if he places his thumb behind the handle. (Most of the top-ranking players, too, use this grip on the racket.)

The stance. The stance in hitting a backhand is similar to a left-handed batter's stance in baseball. Stand facing the left line with your feet comfortably apart, your racket gripped properly and hanging loosely at your right side. Now advance your right foot a comfortable distance forward and point the left foot slightly toward the base line. This is the set stance that will be used throughout the instructions on the backhand.

Fig. 26. The backswing for the backhand stroke.

The point of contact. The point of contact for the backhand, or the point at which the racket strikes the ball, is just forward of the right hip (Fig. 25). Your racket at this point should be facing directly toward the net, and a ball struck at this point will fly straight back over the net. Your arm should be perfectly straight at the moment of impact.

The backswing. As in the forehand, a wind-up is unnecessary, the backswing being a very simple straight one (Fig. 26). With the proper grip on the racket, hold the racket at the point-of-contact position, just forward of your right hip and at waist level. Place your left hand at the throat of the racket. Now sweep your racket sideward, backward, and slightly upward from the point of contact, drawing it back with the left hand. Place the racket directly over the 5 o'clock position on your imaginary clock face, with the racket head about on a level with your shoulders (Fig. 27). (Again, you are hitting toward 12 o'clock on the clock face.) Your right arm should be slightly bent, with your wrist turned back only slightly and the racket face tilted backward slightly.

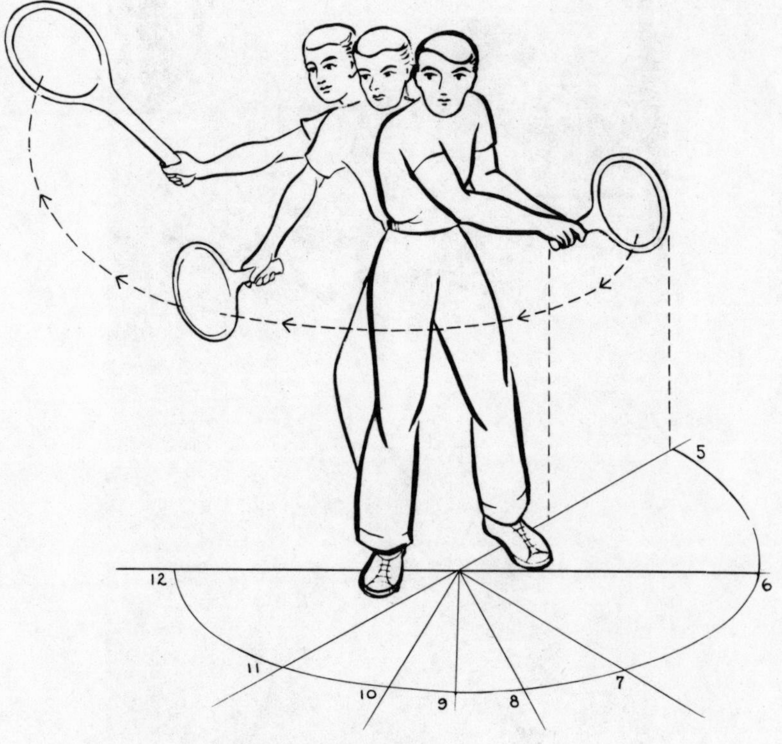

Fig. 27. The backhand swing.

(The tilting back of the racket face, or of the top edge, insures a firm wrist throughout the swing.) With your racket in this position, turn your body at the waist so that the right shoulder is slightly closer to the left side line than is the left shoulder. This is the first fixed point of the backhand. Your weight should be on the rear or left foot.

The shift of weight. With the racket back to the fixed position, over 5 o'clock on the face of the imaginary clock, merely step toward the left net post with your right foot and transfer your weight from the left to the right foot.

The body pivot. There is a definite body pivot in the backhand stroke, but it is not so great as in the forehand stroke. Your body at the beginning of the swing does not face directly toward the left side line but rotates backward slightly toward the base line. From this position, it pivots forward until the right shoulder points in the direction of the shot. The pivot should follow just after the shift of weight.

The forward swing. Release the left hand from the racket throat, and swing the arm and racket toward the net by dropping the racket head slightly to waist level, and then swing it through the point of contact and

Fig. 28. The finish position of the backhand swing.

upward to head height until the racket is at the 1 o'clock position. This brings the racket, arm, and shoulder in line at the 1 o'clock position and completes the full forward swing. As the racket moves forward, your right elbow should move away from your body and should be reaching for the net at the finish of the stroke (Fig. 28). The secret of producing a rhythmical stroke lies in smoothly combining the three elements of body pivot, shift of weight, and arm movement.

The complete backhand swing. After you and your Buddy have gone through the previously mentioned Seven Points of Form several times, you are ready to put them together into the complete backhand swing.

Grip the racket as previously described for the backhand, assume the proper stance, and place the racket at the point-of-contact position, just forward of your right hip. Now place your left hand on the racket throat, and keeping the wrist firm and turning the top edge of the racket backward slightly, sweep the racket backward, upward, and sideward from the point of contact. This will place it directly over the 5 o'clock position, which is the racket-back position, on the imaginary clock face. Your right arm should be fairly close to your body and the weight should be on your left foot with the shoulders turned so that the right shoulder is closer to the left side line than the left shoulder. The full forward swing is now made by releasing the left hand from the racket and swinging the right arm and the racket forward, shifting the weight, and pivoting in a coordinated movement to the finish position. As in the forehand, during the swing your knees should be bent just enough to provide the necessary knee action for a smooth body pivot.

You and your Buddy should spend considerable time practicing the swing, checking each other as you do so. Each of you should go through the swing time and time again and, as in the forehand, emphasize the two fixed points, the racket-back position, and the finish position.

Here are some things to keep in mind when practicing the backhand:

1. Be sure you assume the proper sideways stance and get your body well turned to the side so that the right shoulder is closer to the left side line than is the left shoulder. Many beginners try to hit backhands from a position in which they are facing the net a little bit too much. The shoulders must be turned in order to insure a full swing.

2. Be sure to turn the top edge of the racket backward slightly during your backswing and keep it that way during the entire swing. This insures the firm wrist that is necessary to a good backhand.

3. Don't "quit" too soon during your swing. Many beginners keep the wrist firm until just before contact with the ball is made. They then let the wrist flop and the racket head drop at the finish position. Keep your wrist firm throughout the swing and finish with the racket head held high above the wrist and the racket firmly gripped.

4. Make sure that your right elbow moves away from your body, out toward the net as the ball is hit, and not toward the right side line. This will insure the proper follow through.

5. Remember the three check points:
   a. racket-back, at 5 o'clock
   b. point of contact, at 9 o'clock
   c. finish position, at 1 o'clock.

Step 2: Hitting a tossed ball

After you and your Buddy have learned the correct backhand swing, you should begin work on hitting a tossed ball on the backhand. This step is similar to the tossed ball step for the forehand and can be learned in the same manner, that is, with the tosser standing against the fence and the hitter standing about ten paces away from him and hitting the tossed balls back to the tosser. Here again, the tosser should check the hitter carefully, making whatever suggestions he thinks necessary to improve the stroke. The hitter should strive to hit the ball directly back to the tosser so that the tosser can catch the balls without moving his feet. Practice this drill first by hitting from a sideways position (the correct stance) until you can hit ten balls in a row back to the tosser. After you have learned this, hit from a waiting position, in which you face the tosser and must turn into a sideways position as the ball is tossed. Ten in a row and you have passed another test! Record your score on each of these tests on the Score Chart in the back of the book.

You can vary the drill somewhat when you are hitting from a waiting position by having the tosser mix up his tosses so that he tosses some balls to your forehand and some to your backhand. You can then practice turning from a waiting position to either the forehand or backhand sideward position. While waiting for the toss to be made, you should hold the racket handle in the forehand grip, while resting the racket throat lightly in your left hand. If the ball comes to you on your forehand side, you merely release the left hand, turn to a sideways position, and stroke the ball, using the grip you already have on the racket. If the ball comes to you on your backhand, you must, of course, turn and change grips at the same time and then complete the backhand swing.

Many beginners have difficulty in changing from the forehand to the backhand grip because they hurry too much while changing. They don't realize how much time they actually have to make the change. During the tossed ball drills, if the balls are tossed slowly, you have sufficient time to turn and change grips without hurrying, and on the court during actual play, when the ball is in the air for a longer period of time, you again have sufficient time to change grips.

If you have difficulty making the change of grips, spend a little time practicing it, shifting several times from the forehand to the backhand and back again to the forehand without swinging the racket. Rest the throat of the racket lightly in your left hand, and use your left hand to help you change your right hand from the forehand to the backhand grip.

Practice changing grips for some time, looking at your hand as you do so. After some experience, of course, the change becomes automatic, and then you can feel it and do it without having to look at the racket.

Step 3: Running to hit a tossed ball

This step can be learned as the forehand step was learned. If you are hitting, you should stand on the base line, midway between the side lines. Your Buddy should stand ten paces from you, toward the net, on your left side line. The toss should be made so that the ball travels parallel to your left side line and bounces to a level about even with your waist. You turn from the waiting position, run to the side line, and stroke the ball when you get there. The footwork should be the same as was used in the forehand drill, that is, short skipping steps should sometimes be taken in order to end in the proper position. Here again, as in the forehand, after some practice on this drill it can be varied somewhat by having your Buddy stand at the center of the court at the net and toss the ball varying distances away from you so that you have to turn, run, and adjust your footwork and body movements to get into the proper position to hit. Once more you can test yourself by trying to hit ten balls in a row back to the tosser.

Hitting a ball that comes directly at you. As we mentioned in the chapter on the forehand stroke, when a ball comes directly at you, you can play it with either a forehand or a backhand stroke. If you decide to use your backhand, swing your left foot backward and toward your right side line and pivot on your right foot. Change your grip from the forehand to the backhand, and take your racket back as you turn. When the ball arrives, step into it with your right foot and complete your stroke.

Hitting high and low backhands. As we mentioned before, while you are playing or rallying you can't depend upon the ball to be at waist level when you hit it. Some shots will have to be made at almost shoe-top level, some at shoulder level, and others at various points between these two levels. You must learn to make the backhand swing at all levels.

For a low backhand shot, one below waist level, you should do the same things that you do on the low forehand shot. Merely bend your knees, so that you bring your waist level down to the level of the ball. Except for the bending of the knees, the stroke is exactly the same as that used on a waist-level ball. On very low shots, those just off your shoe tops, you'll have to bend your knees and drop your racket head slightly in order to get it down to the ball.

When hitting a high backhand, hold the racket and arm during the backswing so that the racket head is as high as you judge that the ball will be when you hit it. The follow through will not be upward, in this case, but straight ahead, or flat. Be sure to turn your body well around to a sideways position when hitting a high backhand.

Step 4: Rallying

After you have learned to run and hit the backhand, you are ready to practice using the stroke during a rally.

You and your Buddy should stand on opposite sides of the net, about 2 feet behind the base line and midway between the side lines, just as you did when rallying on the forehand. In order to start the rally one player should drop and hit a forehand (the feeder stroke), aiming at his Buddy's backhand. The ball should then be played on the backhand, on the first bounce, if possible. Here, too, you will have to move forward or backward on the court, or to the left or the right, depending on the length or direction of your Buddy's shot, in order to get into the proper position to hit the ball. Don't go too far forward, however, to play a very short ball. Wait for it to come back to you and play it on the second bounce. If your Buddy's feeder shot is a little off direction and comes to you on your forehand side, catch the ball, drop and hit it (using the forehand stroke), and then start the rally over.

While rallying on the backhand, don't try to hit the ball so hard that you can't control it. Try, at first, merely to get the ball back deep to your Buddy's backhand so that he can practice his stroke, also. When you and he can each hit ten backhands in a row without missing, you have passed the test for this stage.

When you have learned to control the ball fairly well when rallying on the backhand, you can then practice keeping it in play by rallying both forehands and backhands. Use the forehand feeder stroke to start the rally, but then use either the forehand or backhand drive, whichever is necessary, to keep the ball in play. It's fun to see how many times you and your Buddy can hit the ball before one of you misses. Try it, counting each hit, and see how long you can keep a rally going. Two top-ranking women players one day kept a rally going, just for fun, and each hit the ball more than 50 times before one of them missed!

5

The Serve Is Your Big Gun

The serve, as we have mentioned previously, is the stroke that is used to put the ball in play during an actual game. A survey of a number of top-flight players would reveal a wide variety of styles of serving, as is true also with ground strokes. Many of these styles have excellent results.

Most of the top-notch players have strong, fast, powerful serves, which they can get in quite regularly. They use their big serves to win points outright, to force errors from their opponents, or to force a weak return which they follow with an aggressive volley or drive.

A player with a really good serve has a tremendous advantage over his opponent while serving. Because he is allowed to hit two serves for each point, he can take chances when serving the first ball, and really "knock the cover" off it, trying for a hard-hit winner. If he misses the first serve, he still has another serve coming, which he can hit more carefully.

So great an advantage has the server, in high-level play, that he expects to "hold" his serve, that is, win the game when he is serving, about eight times out of ten. Rarely does the receiver expect to "break through" and win his opponent's serve. Many championship matches follow the pattern of each server "holding" his serve for several games, with one player finally breaking through, to win his opponent's serve and the match.

A powerful serve is not easy to learn. It is one of the most difficult strokes in the game to master unless you get off to a good start when first learning to make the stroke. Proper form must be learned while hitting an easy ball, and then speed, placement, and spin can be added to develop the "big" serve.

Nothing is as discouraging, when playing tennis, as a server not being able to get the serve in the court. A server who frequently serves double faults spoils the game not only for himself but for his opponent as well. For the beginner, then, the serve should be looked upon merely as a means of putting the ball in play; he should hit his serve easy while using proper form.

THE SHORT-SWING SERVE

We like to teach beginners a simple, short-swing serve during their first few lessons. There are a few differences between a beginner's short-swing serve and the expert's full-swing serve, but there are a lot of similarities, too. Some things which are learned during the short-swing (the toss of the ball, for example, and timing and judgment) are also used in the full-swing. Once you have learned them while using the short-swing, it is an easy task to apply them to the full-swing.

Because we think beginners should learn quickly to get their serves in, and because the short-swing serve is easy to learn, we teach it to our pupils. After only one or two practice sessions, some beginners know how to hit their serves in quite regularly and are able to add some speed and placement to their serves.

The grip. Assume the same grip as was used in the forehand groundstroke (shake hands with the racket).

The stance. Stand sideways to the net, then point your feet at the right net post, keeping them comfortably spread. In singles you are allowed to stand between the center mark and the singles side lines, and in doubles between the center mark and the doubles side line. We suggest you stand about 3 feet to the side of the center mark when serving. You must, of course, stand behind the base line.

The point of contact. The racket should meet the ball at the height of your reach directly over or slightly forward of the front or left foot.

The toss. The ball should be held lightly in the fingers of the left hand and should be tossed upward directly over or slightly forward of your left foot. Your left arm should be dropped slightly from the waiting position, then moved upward with your elbow being kept straight. The ball should be released as your left hand passes in front of your face. You should toss the ball just slightly higher than you are able to reach with the top edge of your racket and in such a manner that, if you were to let the ball drop to the ground, it would strike the ground about 3 or 4 inches in front of your left foot. The ball will then be struck just after it starts to drop. Don't make a jerky toss, but let your left hand follow through after the ball until your left arm is fully extended.

Practice the toss several times by placing a racket on the ground directly in front of your left foot. As you toss the ball, let it drop to see if it drops directly on the face of the racket on the ground. Most beginners toss the ball too far behind them. You will probably have the same difficulty, but with the target-racket on the ground to guide you, you can easily learn to toss the ball in the correct manner.

The swing. In starting the swing for the half-swing serve, stand as described above and extend the racket toward the net. Hold it so that the racket head is about on a level with your face and your wrist about on a level with your chest (Fig. 29). Hold the ball in your left hand and

Fig. 29. The starting position for the serve.

rest your left hand lightly against the racket handle. Swing the racket head back over your right shoulder and let it fall slightly behind your back, keeping your right elbow at shoulder height. At the same time, your left hand should be dropping slightly from the waiting position, down against your left thigh. Without pausing, move your left arm upward and toss the ball as described in the preceding paragraph. As the ball reaches its maximum height, "whip" the racket upward and forward as far as you can reach comfortably. You should "break" your wrist at the top of the swing by flipping the racket head forward, over your wrist. Shift your weight from the rear foot to the front foot during the course of the stroke. Try to hit the ball flat when you use the short-swing serve, and don't try for too much speed. Remember, the stroke is used merely to put the ball into play.

When you are just beginning to learn the short-swing serve, we suggest that you practice by serving against a fence. If you stand five or six paces from a fence surrounding a tennis court and serve against the fence, most of the balls will bounce directly back to you, and you will have to spend very little time chasing them. Practice for a considerable time in serving against the fence before you try to hit the balls into a service court. You must get the feel of the toss and the swing before you try to get direction and speed on the ball. After you have acquired the feel of the swing and the toss you can move on to the court and, standing behind the base line with whatever balls you have available, practice the short-swing serve there, trying to hit the ball into the proper service court.

THE FULL-SWING SERVE

After you have learned the short-swing serve, you should then begin practicing on the full-swing serve. The waiting position, the grip, the stance, the point of contact, and the toss for the full swing are exactly the same as they were for the short-swing serve. The serve is begun by holding the racket out toward the net so that your wrist is at chest level and the racket head is level with your face. Your left hand, in which you hold the ball, should be resting against the handle of the racket. From this starting position, swing your left arm downward against your left thigh and, at the same time, swing the racket head down past your right knee and over your shoe tops, then backward away from the net. The racket should continue to move backward and upward until its head is about shoulder high, behind you, and pointing away from the net (Fig. 30). From this position, bring your arm forward in a throwing motion by dropping the racket head behind your back in a small looping swing and then whipping the head upward and forward as far as you can reach comfortably. Your left hand, in which you hold the ball, should move upward to toss the ball just as the racket starts to move up after it passes your shoe tops. Your arms should move down and up together. The toss should be directly in front of your left foot and, as in the half-swing serve, about as high as you can reach with the top edge of the racket, so that the ball is struck just after it starts to drop. During this whipping or throwing motion of the racket head, "break" the wrist at the top of the swing so that the racket whips forward and leads the arm to

Fig. 30. The full-swing serve.

the finish position, which is forward of the body directly in front of the shoe tops. Shift your weight from the rear foot to the front foot during the course of the stroke. The forward thrust of your body will cause your left heel to rise from the ground during the forward swing, and your right foot will slide forward with its toe scraping along the ground as it does so. (The rules of tennis require that you keep one foot on the ground when serving, so try not to jump during your swing.)

The type of serve that should be learned first when using a full-swing is the one in which you hit the ball on its top right side so that the ball is spinning in a sideways direction when it leaves your racket. This sideways spin on the ball will cause it to curve to your left during its flight, just as a ball curves in baseball when a pitcher throws it. This type of serve is called a "slice" serve; it is the basic serve of practically all tennis players' games.

To get the proper spin on the ball, we suggest that in serving you imagine that there is a clock face on the ball and that you strike the ball a glancing blow with the racket, meeting the ball at 2 o'clock. The racket should hit the ball on the top right side.

Practicing your serve

The best procedure in practicing your serve is to start by serving against a wall or the fence around the tennis court. Stand five or six paces from the fence and hit the balls directly against it. In most cases the balls will bounce directly back to you, or pretty close to you, so that

(photo courtesy the *Athletic Journal*)

Vic Seixas, American Davis Cup star, hitting a full-swing serve—the American twist.

you won't have to spend a great deal of time chasing them. After you have acquired the feel of the full-swing serve, have good timing and judgment, and are able to toss the ball fairly accurately, it is time for you to move out to the court.

When practicing the serve on the court, you and your Buddy should get as many balls as you can and, placing them in a box or a basket, stand on the base line to the right of the center mark and place the box between you. Take turns, then, in hitting a serve—one of you hitting while the other watches him and suggests corrections to him. You will be serving, of course, to your left, if standing to the right of the center mark. Hit your entire supply of balls, then pick them up together, and resume hitting after you have retrieved them all. Serving in this manner is excellent practice because if you spend just a few minutes doing this, each of you will hit as many, if not more, serves than if you were to play an entire set, which would take much more time. Don't try to hit your serves too hard at first. Merely try to get the ball in the court, working to develop the feel of the stroke and the feel of the racket as it strikes the ball. Don't spend too much time serving from the right of the center mark to your left, but vary your practice by moving to the left of the center mark and serving to your right into the backhand court.

Combining serve and drive practice

After both of you have learned to control the serve pretty well, you can combine serving practice with groundstroke practice. One of you can serve and the other can stand on the opposite side of the net, at the junction of the base line and side line, and practice returning the serve (use your forehand or backhand drive, depending on which side the ball comes to you). The server should work on steadiness first; then he should try to place the ball to the corners of the service court.

You should stand about 2 or 3 feet from the right of the center mark when serving to the right court and practice serving the ball so that it travels almost parallel to the center service line and goes to your Buddy's backhand. In actual singles play—in doubles, too, for that matter—most of your serves should be made to this position, or to your opponent's backhand. The angle serve, in which the server aims to his left so that the ball lands in the service court close to the junction of the service line and and singles side line, should also be practiced. This ball, of course, will go to your Buddy's forehand and give him practice in returning the serve with the forehand stroke. A good server is able to hit the ball in both places, down the center to the receiver's backhand or to the left, to the receiver's forehand. During actual play he will vary his serves frequently, keeping the receiver guessing as to whether the ball will come to the forehand or the backhand side.

The same drill should be practiced with the server standing to the left of the center mark and serving to his right, or to his opponent's backhand court. Here the server should stand 4 or 5 feet to the left of the center mark and spend most of his time trying to get the ball wide to his right to the receiver's backhand. The serve down the center, however, should also be practiced. The receiver here can practice returning the serve, using both the forehand and backhand groundstrokes.

Additional serving practice can be given to a player if he needs extra work on his serve by having him play a set and letting him serve every game throughout the set. This is a practice procedure that we use quite often in working with our pupils and one that we have found to be quite helpful. We sometimes also let a player hit three serves for every point instead of the regulation two, to give him additional service practice.

If you have a good service stroke but tend to tighten up, or "choke up," on the second ball after you have missed the first ball, you can learn to get over this fear of missing by playing a set and limiting yourself to one serve for each point. Because you'll realize that you must get every serve in, you will not overhit the ball and you will soon learn to serve at a medium speed (one with a high degree of safety), taking no chances as you hit the ball. Once you have learned to get most of these one-ball serves in, you will acquire confidence in your serve and you will be well on your way to getting over the fear of double faulting whenever you play a regulation game.

THE FLAT SERVE

After you have learned to hit a fairly good slice serve (one that you can get in quite regularly), you should begin work on adding speed to your serve by swinging hard and hitting the ball flat or with a very small amount of spin on it. A hard-hit flat serve, often called a "cannonball serve," is used by a majority of good players as a first serve. It is a risky type of serve because the ball, as it leaves the racket, has no spin on it and doesn't drop as it crosses the net. It must be hit low so that it barely clears the net, which results in a small margin of safety.

The stroke for a flat, hard serve is the same as that used in a slice serve, with this exception: at the moment of impact as the racket strikes the ball, your wrist should be turned so that the ball is hit flat or directly on the 12 o'clock position of a clock face on the ball. This slight turning of the wrist is the only change in the swing.

Practice the flat serve after you have learned the slice. Use the methods that we have suggested earlier for practicing the slice service. When playing a game use the flat serve only on your first ball because it is a risky serve, one that you are not expected to get in too often. On the second ball, which you must get in or double fault, use your slice serve, hitting the ball fairly easy.

THE AMERICAN TWIST SERVE

The most difficult of all serves to learn, and the one which you should not worry about until after you have learned the slice and the flat serves, is the American twist serve. In this serve, the racket moves upward and across the ball, imparting top spin to it, which causes it to bounce high when it lands in the service court. The toss for the twist serve should be to your left and slightly behind you so that the ball is struck somewhere in the vicinity of a point directly above your back. The farther to the left you toss the ball, the more you will have to bend your back toward the ball during your swing and the more twist or top spin you will put on the ball. A slight change in the grip from the forehand toward the backhand also aids in imparting spin to the ball.

The twist is an extremely difficult serve, one that takes a lot of time to learn. Don't worry about it, however, until after you have learned the slice and the flat serves.

6

Your Drives Can Win

During actual play in a tennis game there are several different uses to which the forehand and backhand drives are put. As a beginning player, you will most frequently use your drives to (1) return your opponent's serve and (2) to move him out of position on the court after the serve has been returned.

RETURNING YOUR OPPONENT'S SERVE

Your normal position when receiving the serve should be a foot or two behind the base line, with your right foot resting just behind the point at which the right singles side line meets the base line if you are receiving the serve in the right, or forehand, court. (If you are receiving the serve in the left, or backhand, court, your left foot should be just behind the point at which the left singles side line meets the base line.) Your stance should be the one we have already described as a waiting position. You should be facing the net and be prepared to move quickly in any direction. Your knees should be slightly bent and your body should be inclined slightly forward, with your weight on the soles of your feet. Hold the racket in the forehand grip and place it in front of your body with the racket throat resting lightly in your left hand.

As your opponent's serve comes toward you, decide quickly which way you have to play it—forehand or backhand. He won't be serving hard if he, too, is a beginner, so you will have plenty of time to turn from a waiting position to a sideways one to make whatever stroke is necessary. If the ball comes directly at you, you will have to turn away from it to use either your forehand or backhand stroke.

The main thing that you should have in mind when returning the serve is to get the ball back into the court. The best place to hit it is deep so that it lands at least 5 or 6 feet from the baseline and bounces to your opponent's backhand. Many beginning players—and advanced players, too, for that matter!—make the mistake of trying to do too much with their service returns. They try to hit the ball too hard or place it too close to the side lines or base line and thus miss the shot. Hit the ball easy, so that it clears the net by 3 to 6 feet and lands deep in your opponent's court, preferably on his backhand. Get the ball back in play and give your opponent a chance to miss the next shot—don't give him the point by missing the return of serve.

As soon as you have made the service return, move quickly to the center of the court, using short, quick, sideward skipping steps as you do so. By the time your shot gets back to your opponent, you should be directly behind, or near, the center mark, in a waiting position, prepared to move in whatever direction is necessary to get to your opponent's next shot. You should return to this position after every shot. On some occasions, if your return of service is hit fairly hard, you may not get back to the center of the court. Move as close to the center as you can, however, before your opponent hits the ball—then stop as he hits, regardless of where you may be in the court, and take the waiting position. You are then prepared to move to the next shot.

You and your Buddy can combine practicing the service return with the serving practice. One of you can serve over and over again, with the other returning the serve. Don't play the point out to its completion. Serve, return serve, and move to the center of the court, then stop the rally. Practice this in both courts, the right and left, taking turns serving and returning the serve.

MOVING YOUR OPPONENT OUT OF POSITION

Your most frequent use of the forehand and backhand drives will be to move your opponent out of position during a rally. Let's assume you have made a good serve and your opponent has returned the ball safely, deep to the middle of the court, and that he has moved to the center of the court after making his service return. Both you and your opponent now are standing a foot or two behind your base lines, about in the center of the court.

Your first thought should be to keep the ball in play and to keep it deep. Any shot of yours which lands deep in the court (about 3 or 4 feet from the base line) is a fairly safe shot if you are in the center of the court behind the base line. Your opponent's return, regardless of how hard he hits the ball, will be in the air for such a long period of time as it travels back over the net that, in most cases, you will have sufficient time to run to the ball and get it back. Keep the ball fairly high, about 3 to 6 feet above the net, and deep, and you'll keep out of trouble.

The best place to hit the ball during a rally is deep to your opponent's weakness. Most players are weaker on their backhands than on their forehands, so your best play, in most cases, is deep to your opponent's backhand. If he returns the ball deep to your court, hit it back deep again, waiting for him to miss completely or to make a weak or short return. By a short return, we mean a ball that you can play from 3 to 6 feet inside your base line.

When he does make a weak or a short return—one that lands short in your court and which you are able to play about waist level on your forehand—hit it low, about 2 feet above the net, and to a corner of the court preferably away from your opponent. Try to make him run to the ball. Because you made your shot from inside your base line and because you hit it low, the ball will be in the air only for a short period of time, and he will have difficulty in getting into position to play it. If he gets to the ball at all, he will be forced to make a defensive shot, one that should give you very little difficulty and which you can hit to the opposite corner to keep him running and off balance.

You and your Buddy can learn how to win points through use of your forehand and backhand drives in the following manner: Stand at opposite sides of the court, a foot or two behind the center mark. One of you can use the feeder stroke to start a rally, then play out the point, bearing in mind the principles about keeping the ball in play, keeping it deep, and merely waiting for a short ball. You can play a little game that many youngsters have found to be fun by limiting your court to the area between the side lines and the base line and the service line. Any ball that lands inside the service line is out, as is one that lands beyond the side lines or the base line. No serve is used, the feeder stroke being used to start the rally. Ten points make up a game. This game, sometimes called *the deep court game*, is excellent practice for learning how to keep the ball deep and in play. It is a game that is often used by good players for brushing up on their ability to keep the ball deep.

LEARNING TO HIT PLACEMENTS

When playing the deep court game or rallying during the course of a regular game, you have to be able to place the ball to various parts of the court in order to move your opponent out of position, or to cause him to miss his returns. Good tennis players rarely "just hit the ball back." They almost always have a definite purpose in mind when hitting the ball.

Usually, as we mentioned, this purpose is to move their opponent around the court in order to keep him off balance and to force him to make a defensive shot, or to hit to a hole or an opening for a winner. In the early stages of your tennis career, you should try only to get the ball back and keep it in play. When you have learned to play a steady type of game, you should start working on accuracy, or the ability to place the ball to various parts of your opponent's court.

There are two general types of placement in tennis: Cross court shots and down-the-line shots. Almost every groundstroke you hit, with the exception of a purely defensive shot, will be some type of cross court or down-the-line shot.

A forehand cross court shot is one which a player hits from a forehand corner diagonally across the court to his opponent's forehand corner. A forehand down-the-line shot is hit from the forehand corner to the opponent's backhand corner, with the ball traveling approximately parallel to the right side line. A backhand cross court travels from the backhand corner to the backhand corner, and a backhand down-the-line travels from the backhand corner to the forehand corner, parallel to the left side line.

The method of stroking the ball when hitting cross court or down the line is only a little different from the one you learned when hitting a tossed ball directly back to your partner. A slight change in the point of contact is the only difference. The point of contact, for a shot straight ahead, is directly opposite your left hip when hitting a forehand. To hit a forehand cross court, merely meet the ball a little forward of your left hip; to hit a forehand down-the-line, meet the ball a little behind the left hip. Backhands are hit cross court or down the line in the same manner, by merely changing the point of contact. Care should be taken when hitting down the line to get your body well into a sideways position and to emphasize the straight-ahead follow-through. With practice and experience you will learn just how much to change the point of contact in order to give direction to your shot.

You and your Buddy can practice placement of your groundstrokes in the following manner; one of you can stand in your forehand corner, the other in his backhand corner. The player in the backhand corner starts a rally by dropping and hitting (feeding) to his Buddy's forehand who can then hit the ball cross court, if he is practicing the forehand cross court shot, or down the line, if he is practicing the forehand down-the-line shot. Don't rally when you first work on this practice drill—merely hit a number of cross courts, then a number of down-the-lines. Alternate feeding and hitting until both of you have acquired the feel of changing the point of contact.

Once you have learned to change your point of contact and can get good direction on your shots, you should move one step farther in the drill: Agree beforehand that one of you (Player A) will hit every ball back to the same spot on the court—the forehand corner, for example. The other player (Player B) then hits both cross courts and down-the-lines, always from the forehand corner. "B" practices his placements while "A" runs back and forth along the base line to retrieve these placements, hitting them all back to "B's" forehand corner. Start the rally by dropping and hitting; then try to keep the ball in play. Change positions on the court from time to time, with "B" playing first on his forehand corner, then in his backhand corner. In this manner he can practice both forehand and backhand placements. After some practice in these positions, let "A" stand in first one corner and then the other and practice his forehand and backhand placements while "B" retrieves these placements.

When practicing these placement shots, don't hit too close to the lines. Aim your cross courts 3 or 4 feet from the side line and your down-the-line shots 3 to 4 feet from the side line and the base line, also. Try to keep the ball deep by hitting it so that it crosses the net by at least 3 or 4 feet.

After you have learned to give direction to your shot, you can vary your placements by hitting short cross courts and short down-the-line shots. You will quickly see how these short cross courts draw your opponent well out of position, provided the ball is well angled. The short cross court, however, is a difficult shot and one that, if not well angled, can easily lead to difficulty. The same is true of the short down-the-line shot. The short shots, however, have their place in tennis and they should be practiced, but only after you have first learned to keep the ball deep.

7

Put Punch into Your Volleys

Previously, it was mentioned that the basic strokes of the game and the strokes around which a sound game must be built are the forehand and backhand groundstrokes (drives) and the serve. Before a player can achieve any degree of success in the game he must have reasonably sound groundstrokes and a fairly good serve.

Good groundstrokes and a good serve alone are not enough, however, for a player to enter into the above-average class of players. He must learn to make the advanced strokes, principally the forehand and backhand volleys, lobs, the overhead smash, and the half-volley, to advance into the championship class where the winning game is played both in the vicinity of the base line and at the net.

THE VOLLEY

The volley (both forehand and backhand) is the stroke used to hit the ball before it bounces ("on the fly"). It is usually made from the forecourt (about 6 to 8 feet from the net) when the player has advanced to this position after having made a deep, well-placed drive (Fig. 31). Its purpose, generally, is to win the point and not merely to keep the ball in play.

The grip. The grips for the volley should be pretty much the same as the grips you use for the ground strokes, at least during the early learning period until you have become accustomed to the fineness of touch and quick movement required to make the stroke. Later, as you begin to feel more at home in the forecourt, you'll find it wiser to use a grip midway between the forehand and backhand groundstroke grips—one that does not necessitate a change of hand position for forehand or backhand volleys.

The stance. The stance at the net (in the forecourt) should, whenever possible, be a sideways one, similar to that used in the groundstrokes. The body faces either the right or the left line for a forehand or backhand volley, respectively.

The swing. The swing for the volley differs from that in the groundstrokes in that there is a very short backswing and practically no follow-through.

The ball is merely punched or jabbed, and the racket head is brought back of the ball with a short arm movement. The forearm and wrist then snap the racket head forward at the ball. The racket should meet the ball out in front

Fig. 31. The volley.

of the body, slightly forward of the front foot, as the weight is shifted forward. The short, sharp jabbing motion of the forearm should result in a very short follow-through.

FIRST STEPS IN LEARNING TO VOLLEY

The best way for you and your Buddy to learn to volley is to use a tossed ball drill similar to the one used in learning the ground strokes. One player tosses and the other hits, with the tosser standing against the fence behind the court and the hitter standing about five paces away from him (Fig. 32). If you are hitting, you should stand in a hitting position (a sideways stance) with a forehand grip on the racket. The racket should be placed at the point-of-contact position which is just forward of your left foot, with the racket head on a level with your face. The racket head then will be above the wrist and arm.

Your Buddy's first few tosses should be made underhand so that the ball merely rebounds off your racket. If your racket is held firmly and if your wrist and forearm are firm, the ball will rebound slowly off the hitting surface of the racket. You should watch the ball carefully and merely block the ball by placing the racket head in front of it.

After some practice at merely blocking the ball and after your timing and judgment have improved, you should begin "punching" the ball by moving the racket head about 2 feet behind the point of contact and then

Fig. 32. Practice drill for the volley.

jabbing it into the ball. The jab or punch should be made with a firm wrist and arm. Work on shoulder-high balls first (the easiest volleys to make), punching the ball directly back to the tosser. This drill should be practiced on both the forehand and backhand sides. The technique is the same on either side, with only the grip and stance differing. For a backhand volley at this stage of learning, use your regular backhand grip and a regular backhand stance.

When you and your Buddy have learned to volley an easily tossed ball, you should move out to the court and volley a dropped-and-hit ball.

When volleying on the court, the correct position at the net is on the center line in a position about midway between the net and the service line. The feeder should stand midway between the side lines just inside the base line. Using the feeder stroke, he should feed his Buddy forehand volleys by hitting the ball about shoulder high to the volleyer. The volleyer should stand in a hitting position facing the side line. As

Fig. 33. Volleying on the court.

the ball approaches, he should take the racket head back behind where he judges the point of contact will be. When the ball arrives, the racket head should then be jabbed forward into the ball.

Don't try placing your volleys at this stage, only try getting them back to your Buddy. Work on this drill until you and he can keep the ball in play with the feeder hitting easy forehand and backhand drives and the volleyer punching back easy volleys. Work on the backhand volley in the same manner, changing positions frequently so that you both get practice on the volleys.

Your next step, of course, is to learn to volley a mixture of forehands and backhands. The feeder can mix up his feeder shots so that the volleyer doesn't know whether the ball will come to his forehand or backhand. The volleyer should stand in a waiting position with his body facing the net, feet well spread, and knees slightly bent, so that he can move quickly in whatever direction is necessary.

Quick movements of the feet are necessary when playing in the forecourt. The outside foot, or the foot farthest from the ball, is swung forward toward the net, then toward the side line as the body turns into a sideways position. For example, if the ball comes to you on your right, swing the left foot forward and turn your body sideways. If the ball comes to you on your left, change grips from the forehand to the backhand and swing the right foot forward to get into a sideways position. The distance you must step with the outside foot and the distance you must reach with your hitting arm depend, of course, on the distance of the ball from your position. On some occasions a short step to the side is all that is needed. On other occasions a wide lunging step is necessary. And on others, when the ball comes directly at you, a forward step alone is all that is necessary.

Not always will you have time to move your feet to the sideways position when volleying. Frequently you will be forced to volley from a waiting position, with the body facing the net (Fig. 33). While the timing and judgment may be difficult in this position, the technique in this stroke is essentially the same as when made from a sideways stance. The ball is merely jabbed or punched, with the wrist and forearm doing most of the work. The body pivot and shoulder turn enter into the volley only to a small degree.

The low volley

When you have both learned to make high volleys, you should practice the low volley, a more difficult shot. Low volleys are more often blocked rather than punched. Because the ball must be hit upward in order to clear the net and because it must land inside the base line, a low volley is not hit as hard as a high volley, which is generally hit downward.

A low volley (below the shoulders) should be undercut slightly by jabbing downward at the ball with the racket head tilted backward slightly. This backward tilt of the racket and the downward jab at the ball will make the ball spin backward as it leaves the racket. This backspin tends to slow down the flight of the ball and keeps it in the court. Except for the downward jab at the ball and the tilting backward of the racket face, the stroke is the same as that used to make a high volley. Take care to bend your knees when making a low volley, however. Be sure to get your body down close to the ground to make the shot much easier for you.

Once you have learned to make forehand and backhand volleys with the regular forehand and backhand grips, the next step is to learn to volley while using a grip midway between the regular forehand and backhand grips. As you move into the advanced levels of play and start playing against better players, not always will you have time to change from the forehand to the backhand grip to make the volley. Quite often during the course of a rally the ball will come back to you so quickly that you won't have sufficient time to make this change. As mentioned, the grip should be midway between the forehand and backhand grips, with the thumb wrapped around the handle. You can practice hitting balls with this grip in the same manner that you practiced hitting volleys with the regular forehand and backhand grips. Start by hitting some tossed balls first. Then have your Buddy feed you both forehand and backhand balls. You return the ball with your new volleying grip. The stroke, when using this grip, is essentially the same as that used with the other grips.

PAVING YOUR WAY TO THE FORECOURT

The approach shot

In top-flight tennis, most of the points are won with a volley or because of an error caused by a volley. An advanced player generally uses his groundstrokes (or drives) to force his opponent out of position and to force him to make a short, weak return. This short return is taken advantage of by being hit fairly hard, deep to a corner of the court. The hitter follows it to the net, after which he makes a volley to finish off the point. This deep-to-the-corner shot is usually referred to as an approach or forcing shot. Its chief purpose is to force the backcourt player wide and deep and to allow the net rusher to move forward in the court to the volleying position.

The approach shot should be made from at least 3 feet inside the base line. To attempt to advance to the net from behind the base line is usually dangerous, because the distance from where the shot is made to the proper net position is so great that the hitter will not be able to advance to this proper volleying position. His opponent's return will catch him somewhere around the service line where it will be necessary to hit a low and weak volley or a half-volley (a purely defensive shot which we shall discuss later).

Be cautious when advancing to the net. A common fault among inexperienced players is to advance to the net behind weak shots. To get to the net safely you should hit strong, deep, forcing approach shots which will make your opponent hit from behind the base line. Your shot should be hit to your opponent's weakest stroke, which, in junior tennis, is usually the backhand.

You must learn not to rush to the net after hitting unless you know that you can reach a position inside the service line from which you can make winning volleys. Knowing your position in the court in relation to the base line will help determine whether you can do that or not. If you are on the base line or inside it when hitting your approach shot, you can probably reach the proper net position behind a deep shot.

In general, you must not rush to the net unless you know that your approach shot was hit with sufficient speed and depth to force your opponent to hit from behind his base line. The greater the distance his passing shot must travel, the more time you will have to intercept it and volley it. Therefore, approach shots should be deep. In junior tennis, *depth, rather than speed, is desirable in approach shots*, although a combination of the two is most desirable.

Practicing the approach shot

Time spent in learning when and how to advance to the net to use your volley will be time well spent. Start a rally from the backcourt with your Buddy, hitting deep forehand and backhand drives. After three or four returns one of you should purposely make a short shot, one that can be returned as a forcing or an approach shot, and which can then be followed to the net.

While rallying during this drill and when actually playing from the backcourt during a game, you should be waiting eagerly for a short return from your opponent. When you get it, pounce on it, moving up quickly so that you hit the ball at waist level or higher, if possible. Drive the ball deep to the corner of your opponent's court and move forward to the volleying position behind the ball. The correct volleying position will vary each time you go up, depending on where your opponent will be when he returns your approach shot. If you hit your approach to his backhand corner, and if he is close to his left-hand alley as he hits the ball, your position in the forecourt should be about 3 feet to the right of your center line—just forward of midway between the net and the service line. If your approach is deep to his forehand corner, your net position should be about 3 feet to the left of your center line.

Be careful when making your approach shot. Don't try to hit the ball too hard or too close to the line. Give yourself some leeway for error. You should not be trying to win the point with this approach shot; it is merely a way for you to get to the net to win with a volley.

When practicing the approach shot, before you hit the ball come to a stop after you have moved forward to get it high on the bounce. Later you can merely slow down a bit as you come forward, and then, afterwards, you can learn to make the shot when running forward, merely skipping into a sideways position to make the stroke and then continuing your advance to the net.

While you are running to the volleying position after you have made your approach shot, follow the line of flight of the ball. Watch your opponent as he winds up to drive the ball back to you. Come to a stop, regardless of where you are on the court, by jumping into the waiting position as he begins to wind up. In the waiting position, your body should be facing the net and your weight should be on the soles of your feet, with the racket held in front of your body. You are then ready to deal with your opponent's return. If he gives you a high ball, volley it, either forehand or backhand, aiming it away from him. If you are fairly close to the net and if you can hit the ball down, punch it fairly hard, trying for a winner. If his return of your approach is low and if you are not as close to the net as you would like to be when you have to deal with his return, use your low volley and get the ball back deep to a corner of his court. Then move forward, following the line of flight of the ball, and get into the proper volleying position. You are then ready for his return.

A good idea to keep in mind when volleying during a match is to angle the high volleys, punching them downward, fairly hard, and to get the low volleys back deep, hitting them easy. Don't try to do too much with a low volley; merely get it back deep.

8

The Lob, the Overhead Smash, and the Half-Volley

Although the drive, the serve, and the volley are the strokes that you will use most often when playing tennis, there are additional strokes which you are sometimes forced to play, and which you must be able to play well in order to have a well-rounded game. Chief among these are the lob, the overhead smash, and the half-volley. They are advanced strokes, somewhat more difficult to learn than the drive, volley, and the serve; nevertheless, you should begin practicing them fairly early in your tennis career.

THE LOB

The lob, both forehand and backhand, is a groundstroke which is generally used to hit the ball over your opponent's head when he is playing at the net (Fig. 34). It appears to be a very simple stroke as the ball is merely jabbed or pushed upward into the air over your opponent's head, out of his reach, and made to land deep into his court. Actually, it is a much more difficult stroke than it appears to be. If the ball is hit too low or too short, of course, your opponent will have no difficulty in returning it, usually for a winner. If it is hit too hard, it will naturally land outside the court beyond the base line.

The lob, used chiefly as a defensive stroke, may also be considered a "time-saver." As such, it enables you to regain good court position when you are forced wide, off the court, by an opponent who has stayed in the backcourt. If used wisely, the lob can win many points for you.

The stroke

The grip and stance for the lob are the same as those used for the drives. The stroke differs from the groundstrokes, however, in that there is very little backswing, very little body pivot and shoulder turn, and a much shorter follow-through. The racket head should be tilted upward as it comes forward, and the short follow-through should be upward, rather than forward, as in the drive.

Practicing the lob

When working with beginning players, we have found that the greatest difficulty is teaching them not to overhit the lob. Most beginners find it difficult to learn the fine "touch" to make good lobs; instead, they tend to

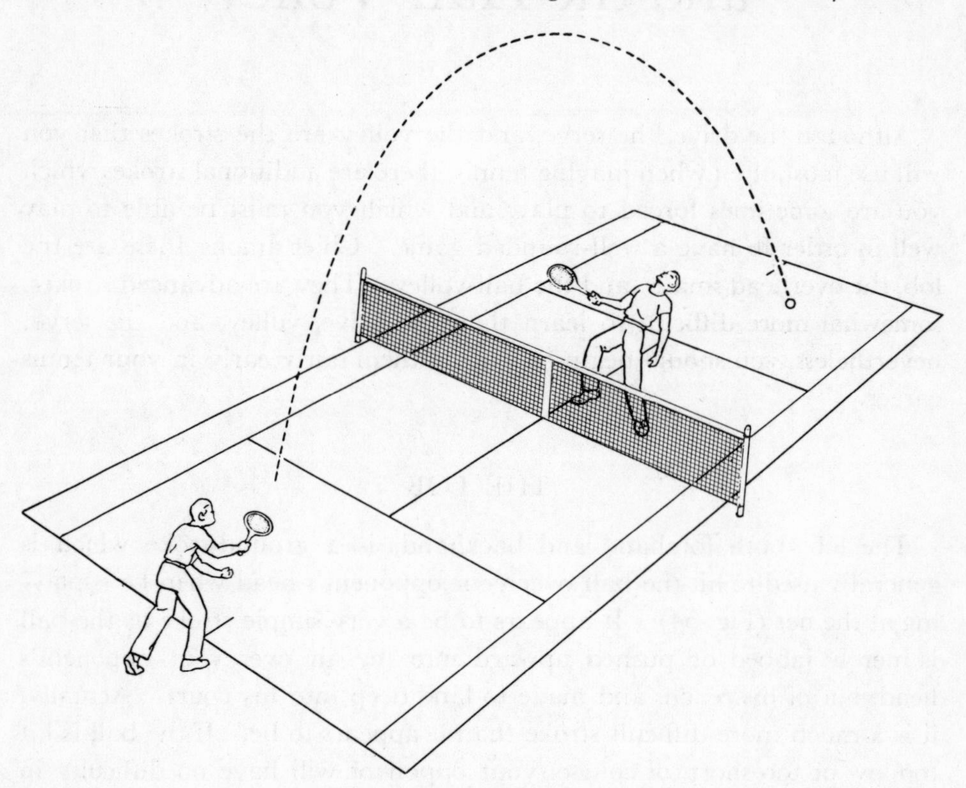

Fig. 34. The lob.

hit most of their shots out, beyond the base line, and too high. Accordingly, we try first to teach them to hit the ball low, and short, and then gradually build up their feel so that they can control the height and depth of the shot. The method we employ can be used by you to learn to make the stroke.

You should begin your lobbing practice by hitting tossed balls. One player should stand at the net, about a foot or so away from it, and toss balls to his Buddy on the opposite base line who lobs the ball over the net man's head. Because the net man is very close to the net, it won't be very difficult for the lobber to make a good lob. It is helpful to the lobber to have the net man hold a racket straight up over his head, to give the lobber an idea of how high the volleyer can reach with his racket. The lobs should be aimed so that they clear the outstretched racket and still land inside the base line. Give each other some forehand and backhand practice in this manner.

Your next step is to use the feeder stroke in setting up balls for the baseliner to lob. The feeder should now stand about 9 feet from the net and drop and hit to the lobber, who should try to lob the ball over the net man's head while keeping it inside the base line. Again, forehands and backhands should be practiced.

The final step is to combine a rally, an approach shot, and a lob. Start a rally with each of you on your base line. Keep the ball in play, using your groundstrokes, until one player gets a short ball which he can hit from inside his base line. He should then make an approach, or forcing shot, deep to a corner of the opposite court and follow it with an advance to the net position. The deep man should then return the approach shot with a lob (Fig. 34).

THE OVERHEAD SMASH

The overhead smash is the answer to the lob. It is the stroke which is used to return a lob which has not cleared a net man (Fig. 35). It corresponds very much to the serve. The grip, the stance, shift of weight, and the swing are almost identical to those used in the serve. The notable difference, however, is in the length of the backswing. The long, sweeping backswing of the serve is not necessary in the overhead smash. The racket head should be brought upward with a short movement of the hitting arm, and the racket should be held somewhat behind your head and back while you are waiting for the ball to descend in its flight.

The racket head should be flipped upward and forward to strike the ball at a point forward of your body. The hitting arm should be straight at the moment of impact.

The hitting motion should be *upward* and forward, and the body weight should shift from the rear foot to the front during the swing.

Short, quick steps are necessary to hit good overheads. As soon as you have determined approximately where the ball will land in the court, move quickly to get directly beneath the ball as it descends and turn your body so that you are in a sideways position, similar to that used in serving. Be prepared to make a few last-second adjustments in your position which might be necessary if you have misjudged the ball, or if the wind causes some change in its flight.

Some high-ranking players take a slight leap upward and backward when hitting overheads. While this makes for a very spectacular shot, it increases the difficulty and timing of the stroke, and should be avoided by all except the most experienced players.

Don't be too eager to win the point with a smash when your opponent lobs to you. If he is a good lobber, you may have to hit three or four good overheads before you can get a short lob which you can "put away."

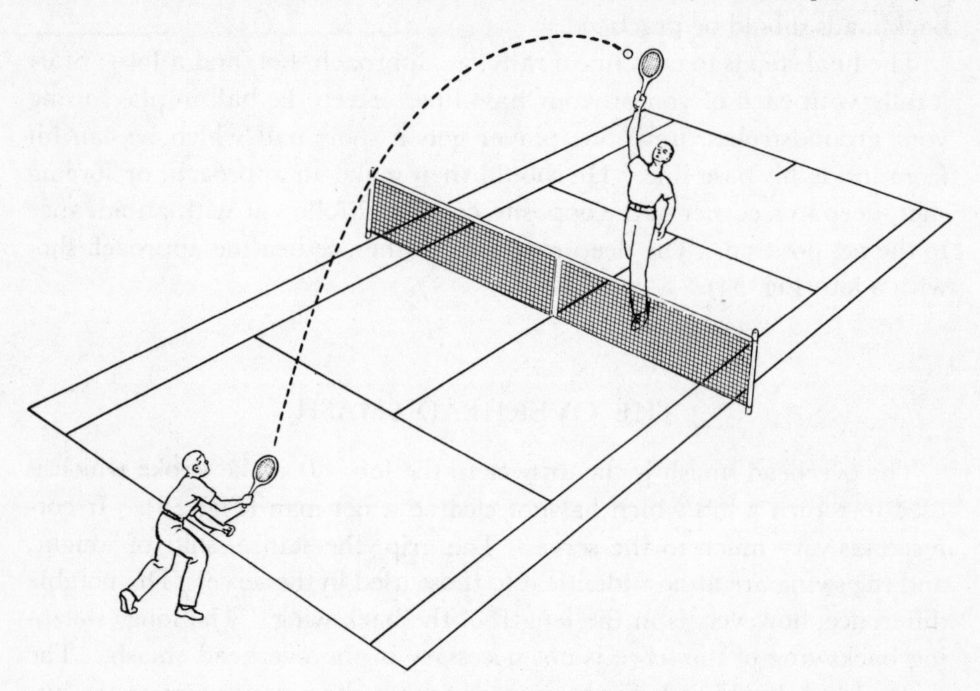

Fig. 35. The overhead smash.

Consider your position in the court when hitting overheads. If you hit from behind the service line the shot should be played safely and hit with only medium speed, followed by a quick return to the volleying position. If you hit from inside the service line, hit it hard, angling the ball to the side of the court. *Get the deep lobs back deep and angle the short ones for winners.*

Practicing the overhead smash

Beginners often get discouraged when they first start to learn to hit overhead smashes. The stroke actually is a simple one, being very much the same as the service stroke, but it is fairly difficult to learn. It involves judgment of where the lob will land in the court and timing of the swinging racket so that the racket meets the rapidly descending ball at the desired, overhead point.

Begin your practice of the overhead by hitting tossed balls. The tosser should stand against the fence, surrounding the court, and toss some lobs directly to the hitter who is standing about ten paces away from the fence. The hitter should use short, quick steps to move directly under the ball as it descends. He should judge its speed and swing the racket so that he hits the ball slightly forward of his front foot and with a straight right arm. The smashes should be hit easy at first, with emphasis placed on learning how to judge the flight of the tossed lob.

You can then move out to the court and again smash some tossed lobs. The tosser here should stand just inside his base line, and the hitter should stand at the regular net position. Aim your smashes directly back at the tosser, stressing footwork practice, judgment, and steadiness.

After you have learned to hit easy tossed balls, you can combine overhead practice with lobbing practice. The feeder, on the base line, can lob to the net man, who smashes the lob. The feeder can then practice lobbing the smash back to the net man. If the lob is deep, it should be smashed deep down the middle; if it is short, it should be smashed to the corners and sides of the court.

THE HALF-VOLLEY

The half-volley is a stroke that is used to return a ball that lands at your feet close to your body. The ball is struck just after it touches the ground (very much like a drop kick in football). The technique of the stroke is very much the same as that for the volley, that is, the same grip and a short backswing are used, with practically no follow-through. The ball is merely blocked by placing the racket head directly behind the point at which you judge it will hit the ground. On some occasions, the racket head should be tilted backwards (as in a low volley) and at other times it should be tilted forward. Whether you tilt it backwards or forward will depend upon your position on the court when you make the shot, the angle of trajectory of the ball as it strikes the court at your feet, and what you are trying to do with the shot. The forward tilt of the racket head will impart top spin to the ball, making it drop short as it crosses the net. A backward tilt will generally result in underspin, causing a ball to stay in the air longer and to carry deep into the court.

If you are going to use the all-court game when you play, you must learn to make a half-volley. While it is primarily a defensive shot, one that is usually used while you are on your way to the net position to volley, it can be an offensive shot, too. It is a difficult shot to learn—one that requires much practice.

Practice drills for the half-volley

You can learn to make the half-volley in the same manner in which you learned to make a volley, that is, you and your Buddy should begin by first of all hitting a tossed ball. The tosser should stand against the fence, and the hitter should stand about four or five paces away from him. The ball should be tossed so that it bounces about a foot or so in front of the hitter and slightly off to his right, so that the hitter can return the ball with a forehand half-volley. Backhand half-volleys can be practiced in this manner, too, if the toss is made to the left of the hitter. After some practice in hitting tossed balls, you should move out to the court to practice the half-volley. One player (the feeder) should stand at the base line and feed his Buddy some half-volleys. His Buddy will be standing on the service line on the opposite side of the net midway between the side lines. At first, the feeding shot should be easy so that it crosses the net just high enough to land at the feet of the man on the service line. Balls should be hit to the forehand of the man on the service line, then to the backhand, and, finally, they should be hit to him in such a manner that he gets a mixture of forehands and backhands.

Practice the half-volley in this manner. It is a stroke which you will not use very often when playing singles (it is used much more often in doubles), but it is one you must be able to make in order to move into higher-class play.

9

Use Your Head *and* Your Racket

The manner in which you stroke the ball in tennis, whether it be a forehand groundstroke, a backhand groundstroke, an overhead smash, or a serve, is often referred to as the "form" or "style" that you use when stroking. In an earlier chapter we told you that the form used by a good player was learned only after a great deal of practice. This style or form, regardless of its type, will be of little value to him in competitive play unless he knows how and when to use it to win a point. He must not only have sound strokes, but also he must know how to use these strokes in such a manner that he derives the greatest benefit from his shots. The winning player knows what he can do well; he also knows, or soon discovers, what his opponent cannot do well, and then exploits his opponent's weakness. He plans his game and forces his opponent to play his plan. The general plan of play in a specific match is referred to as *strategy*. Strategy is merely the manner in which you "use your head" in tennis.

Young, inexperienced players often go out on to the court to play a match with little or no idea of what they are going to do. True, sometimes too little is known of the opponent to plan anything in advance; however, during the first few games a player should attempt to discover his opponent's weaknesses. He should note which shots win for him and which tactics prove most effective. He should then formulate a plan in accordance with what he has discovered and should carry out this plan in actual play. However, a plan should be flexible enough so that, if it proves to be ineffective, it can be changed during a match.

Generally, there are but two basic plans for play in a tennis match. One is to rush to the net and win points by volleying from that position. The other is to remain in the back court and outstroke the opponent from the base line. Since few young players have what is known as an all-court game (that is good ground strokes *and* good volleys), they will usually have to adopt one or another of these plans, depending upon which they can do better. However, by making intelligent use of their strong points, players may combine a little of each plan even though their games are not equally as strong at the net and the back court. For example, hard, accurate groundstrokes, followed to the net, may draw weak shots from an opponent which can be volleyed for winners by even a mediocre net player. In this manner, a player's strong back-court game may strengthen his weak net game.

Regardless of the general plan employed, certain ideas will have to be applied for the plan to succeed. For example, even a very good volleyer will have trouble unless he keeps the ball deep. In short, a player will have to combine good strokes with good use of these strokes to be successful in tennis.

RUSHING TO THE NET

Let us consider the first plan mentioned: rushing to the net to win on volleys. If your strength lies in your volleys, you should attempt to advance to the net as soon as possible. However, if your service is weak it is foolish to follow it to the net. In such a case, it is wiser to wait for groundstrokes to advance to the net. Perhaps your first serve is strong but the second only fair or weak. Then you may go to the net on the first serve, but not on the second. Again, it may sometimes be better for you to "serve your second ball first," provided you have a good spin service with a big hop to the receiver's weakness. Oftentimes, such a medium-paced, well-placed spin service is more difficult for the receiver to handle than a harder flat service. Advancing to the net behind it may be more effective.

When your plan is to advance to the net on groundstrokes, there are fine points to consider also. You should soon discover to what extent you must risk making errors on your approach shots. If your opponent has good passing shots, then you must hit hard and deep to any weakness. If his passing shots are only fair, however, your approach shots need be only of medium pace, thus eliminating some possibilities of errors by you. If the points are going against you, it may be because your approach shots are too weak, and thus your volleys too difficult to make consistently. Another reason may be a bad position at the net which resulted from anticipating a lob that forces you to make difficult low volleys. On the other hand, if the points are won by you, it may be because of your accurate, well-placed approach shots rather than your volleys. Maybe your opponent is missing more than his share of passing shots or setting up easy returns which you can volley for winners.

Knowing how and why points are going one way or another in a match should be a big concern of every player. If you are rushing to the net and winning, you should continue to play your winning style, but at the same time you should be alert for any changes in your opponent's game that may turn the tide. If his passing shots get better, then your approach shots must be made stronger. If his base line game is too good for your net-rushing, it may be wiser for you to stay in the back court and try to draw him to the net, since that is probably where he will feel least at home. This would mean a complete change of play by you. Maybe your back court game, though only fair, would be good enough to win in this manner since your opponent's net game would presumably be only fair, also.

PLAYING FROM THE BACK COURT

When you adopt the steady, back court style of play there are a number of different things to consider. Oftentimes you will be playing against another player who uses the same style, in which case the match will consist of many long rallies with both of you staying in the back court. Then it is generally the player who is better at discovering and exploiting weakness who wins out. Occasionally, your opponent's backhand may be steadier, though not usually stronger, than his forehand. His forehand may be hit harder, but he may also miss it more often. Another device would be to lure him to the net with the intent of passing him for a winner. Since he is a baseliner by choice he probably is weak at the net. To draw him in and away from his favorite base line position would be sound strategy. You should attempt to discover how well your opponent handles speed and spin, and whether he handles each equally well on both the forehand and the backhand. Oftentimes, a mixture of hard and soft shots, a change of pace, and a variety of spins will upset a baseliner's game.

BEATING THE NET-RUSHER

When you are a baseliner playing against a net-rusher, you have other considerations. You must be able to pass the net man or make him miss his volleys more often than you yourself miss from the back court. Your chief concern, then, should be to make the net-rusher's advance to the net as hazardous as possible. This can be done by keeping the ball deep in your opponent's court and to his weakest stroke. Oftentimes much of the sting can be taken out of a net-rusher's game by refusing to let him hit forcing approach shots from inside the base line. When losing points, you should determine whether it is the accurate volleys of the net-rusher or his forcing approach shots which make his net game so effective. It may even be that you are trying to be too accurate on your passing shots and thus missing many of them. At any rate, you should determine the reason points are going against you, and you should change your tactics and strategy accordingly.

The best way to beat a net-rusher is to keep your errors down. Try to make your opponent *win* the point with a volley when he is at the net or advancing to the net. Don't *give* the point to him by trying, and missing, a hard placement. When you are deep in your court, a medium-paced, low-type shot placed either cross court or down the line can be made more consistently than a hard-hit shot. Though not always winning the point outright, this low shot, at the net man's feet, will force him to make a difficult low volley, which he will often miss. Because he is forced to hit up, he won't be able to hit the ball hard. His volley will have to be hit easily and will often land short in your court. You can then step in, get the ball high on the bounce, and drive these short shots past your opponent. You will be hitting them hard either cross court or down the line, and it will be easier than if you were to try to do the same thing from behind your base line.

If your opponent is quick in getting to the net position, the use of the lob will slow him down. Mix in a few lobs with your drives to keep him from coming up too fast. Once he learns that you can lob, he will come up more slowly, to guard against your lob, and it will be easier for you to drive the ball at his feet.

Quite often your opponent will "crowd the net," moving close to it, to cut off your drives before they drop, or to cut off your hard-hit passing shots. Here, too, a few lobs, mixed in with your drives, will force him to stay back, and again it will be easier to drive to his feet or to pass him. A mixture of lobs and low drives will often be enough to upset a net-rusher's plans.

You may find, when your lob is short, that your opponent is able to smash it away for a winner. You will have to increase the depth of your lob and hit it a little higher. A high, deep lob is a difficult one for a junior player to smash, because few junior players have really good overheads.

Learn various methods of returning the service

As soon as possible in a match, you should discover how you can best deal with your opponent's serve. If it has a high bound which carries deep and off the court, it may be wise to stand inside the base line and take it on the rise. If your opponent follows his serve into the net, you could take it on the rise in order to drop returns at his feet, and force him to hit up with a defensive volley. A fine point to consider here will often prove effective in junior tennis: when handling fast serves, or good spin serves that are followed to the net, it may be wiser for you to refrain from hitting for the side lines. Quite often a low return, hit on the rise, directly at the net-rusher's feet will draw a weak volley which will be a setup for a passing shot (Fig. 36).

If the serve is not difficult to handle, you should discover whether or not you can make accurate forcing shots when returning it. If so, it may be wise to follow the service returns into the net. Most likely, though, the serve will be sufficiently hard to make forcing returns difficult. It is wiser merely to block the shot deep to the corners and wait for a more opportune moment to go to the net.

Regardless of what general plan of play you use during a match, there are certain principles which, if followed, will make you a better player.

Hit into levels above the net. You will profit if you develop the habit of "hitting into levels." Besides hitting every shot to a definite area in the opponent's court, you should strive to make the ball cross the net at a certain height. The height or level above the net for each shot will vary, depending upon the type and the purpose of the shot.

In general, there are three levels into which the ball can be hit. The first and lowest level is that which extends from the top of the net to a foot or two above it. All very hard shots, short cross court shots, passing shots, and shots to the net man's feet should be hit into this level.

The next level includes the medium heights of from 2 to 5 feet above the net. All rallying shots, slow shots intended to give time for recovery and return to proper position, and accurately placed shots to the corners should be hit into this level.

The third level is that which extends from 5 to approximately 30 feet above the net. It is the level into which you should hit lobs.

The young player's shots should generally be hit into the medium level, because that is the safest height for both steadiness and depth. Your passing shots, however, should be as low as possible to force the net man to volley up, should he reach the ball. Therefore, they should be hit into the lowest level. To increase the depth of shots, the ball can be hit either harder or higher, or both. You then should find the right height and proper speed at which you are most consistent and effective for each type of shot.

Fig. 36. The return of service.

U. S. Davis Cup star Vic Seixas returns the serve from the backhand court. His receiving position is inside the base line, where he plays the ball early while it is rising.

Do not sacrifice control for speed. Junior players are often impatient to win a point. They must be taught that accuracy rather than speed leads to winning in junior play. An accurate, steady base line game will draw more errors from your opponent than wild, uncontrolled speed. Striving for winners by hitting hard from behind the base line is not percentage tennis. The chances for error are too great. It usually takes two, three, or even four good shots to win when hitting from the back court. Therefore, medium-paced, accurately placed shots are safer. They will be made consistently and still pave the way for an advance to the net, by drawing weak shots from the opponent.

Even approach shots, which are meant to be followed to the net, are not usually intended to win the point outright. Cutting down on the number of errors made from them, even at the sacrifice of speed, will pay dividends provided the ball is kept deep.

Give the opponent credit for his good shots. It is foolish for you to try to make winning shots when returning strong shots of your opponent. Instead, you should be content to keep the ball in play with a deep return placed so as to leave yourself least vulnerable. Few junior players can make good, hard shots consistently. Therefore, it is wiser to be patient and wait for weak shots from which to make forcing, aggressive shots.

Develop an accurate, steady base line game. In junior play, especially, a steady back court game will pay dividends. If you volley well, you should have in mind getting to the net as soon as possible. But you must be able to keep the ball in play from the back court until the

(photo courtesy of the *Athletic Journal*)

The server is probably rushing to the net behind his serve, so Seixas merely uses a short swing to chop the ball back to the server's feet.

opportunity to go to the net is presented to you. Having the type of game which enables you to wait for the proper *shot* on which to advance to the net makes playing at the net much easier. In that respect, a steady base line game strengthens a net rushing game at the junior level of play.

Keep the ball deep. You must also develop depth and speed along with steadiness to prevent your opponent from making good forcing shots which can be followed to the net. Many junior players attempt to win their points at the net, but few take the proper precautions about advancing to it. If a man hitting from the backcourt keeps his shots deep, careless net-rushers will often attempt to hit and advance to the net from behind their base line. It is difficult to make forcing approach shots from this position. Often the approach shot will be weak or inaccurate. Most important is that the distance from the hitting position to the proper net position will be too great for the net-rusher to cover. Consequently, he will be caught out of position. Passing him, or dropping a shot at his feet, will then be a comparatively easy matter for the base line player.

10

Doubles Can Be a Lot of Fun

In the opinion of many tennis fans, the most exciting and entertaining kind of tennis to watch is a doubles match, in which two good, fairly evenly matched teams oppose each other. Many tennis players prefer doubles to singles, too, for pure fun and enjoyment. The quick, fast exchanges of volleys, when all four players are at the net, and the hard-hit overhead smashes used to return the frequent lobs make for much more spectacular play than that which is generally found in a singles match. Once a player has learned the basic strokes of the game, and has had some experience playing singles, an entirely new and exciting experience awaits him on the doubles court.

The technique of good, high-class doubles play differs considerably from that in singles play. As you have learned, you can win in singles against all but the really top-notch player by playing in the backcourt, relying on your groundstrokes. In doubles, however, when playing against good players, you must be at home in the forecourt; you must be able to volley well and to hit decisive overhead smashes. In addition, a good serve and a good return of serve are necessary to win against a high-class doubles team.

Because two players make up a team in doubles, and because the court is only a trifle wider than it is in singles, it is difficult to win points by placements from the backcourt. Since it is customary for partners to play a side-by-side position in doubles, each player on a team has only a narrow area to cover. Each is responsible for covering, approximately, only the area of the court bounded by the doubles sideline and a line drawn down the center of the court. One player covers one side of the court, and his partner covers the other side. The area for which each player is then responsible is much narrower than a singles court, so only the hardest hit, most accurately placed drive will win for a team if their opponents are deep in their court. A team must get to the net position and use volleys to win, punching the ball deep down the middle of the court, between their opponents, or angling it sharply to the left or right side of the court.

The net position is the attacking position and each team tries to get to the net as quickly as possible. Here's how it is usually done by experienced players: The server's partner takes up a position at the net, 6 to 8 feet from it, and about 4 feet from the doubles side line, in front of the receiver of the serve. He is then responsible for covering the area bounded by the doubles side line and, approximately, the center line. The server, immediately after he hits the serve, rushes forward and joins his partner at the net, covering the area bounded by the center line and the other side line. He and his partner are then ready to volley or smash their opponent's returns.

The receiver's partner plays back on the base line, on his side of the court, *or* close to the service line, again on his half of the court. Where he plays depends upon how well his partner can return the serve. If the serve is not too difficult to handle, and if the receiver can return it in such a manner that the server must make a low volley as he runs forward, the receiver's partner plays on or near the service line. If the serve is difficult to handle, and if the receiver has difficulty returning it low, his partner stands on or near the base line.

The receiver of the serve, if he can handle the serve fairly well, will try to return the ball to the net man's feet to force him to volley up and will then move forward to join his partner, who is waiting for him on the service line. All four players will then be in the forecourt, where the team that volleys best will most often win the point.

If the receiving team stays in the backcourt after the return of serve, they will have to use their groundstrokes to make passing shots or to force their opponents to miss a volley. Here their best shots are low drives at the net man's feet, hard drives down the middle of the court, between the net men, or, occasionally, hard drives down the side of the court. The hard shots, down the middle or down the sides, will win if they are made from well inside the base line; if they are hit from deep in the court, however, and if they are hit too high, so that the net man can volley them downward, they will be volleyed away for winners.

If the drives are hit low, the net men will have to volley up, and will have to hit the volley easy to keep it from carrying out, beyond the base line. The ball is generally kept in play, then, by being volleyed deep to the base line by the net men and by being driven low to the net men by the backcourt players, with each team waiting for the other to make a mistake. A high drive will be volleyed away for a winner by the net men; a short, high-bounding volley will be driven hard between the net men or down the side and followed to the net by the backcourt team, who will then try to win with a volley.

Rallies are seldom long and drawn out in high-class doubles play. Most frequently, a rally consists only of a serve, a return of the serve, and two or three volleys. Frequently, lobs and overhead smashes are used, but in general, volleys, half-volleys, and low drives are the principal strokes used.

To really "go places" as a doubles player, a player must be able to volley well. He must be quick when playing at the net, because the ball is returned quickly to him by his opponents who are also playing at the net. Most of the top doubles players in tennis are amazingly quick during an exchange of volleys. They almost always seem to be able to get the racket on the ball, even when thay have only a split second to do so. A slow-moving volleyer in a high-class doubles match is like a fish out of water; he is helpless and just can't keep the ball in play.

So far we have talked about how good players play top-notch doubles. However, younger players do not always have to follow these ideas. In fact, only highly ranked juniors are capable of using these ideas exactly as they are presented here.

Many players at the high school level have had some success in doubles play despite the fact that they were not exceptionally good volleyers. The reason for this is that high school doubles is not usually as much a volleying game as is top-notch senior doubles. At the high school level, a poor volleyer with good groundstrokes can often team up with a good volleyer to make a good doubles team. Each of them can make effective use of his good strokes by having the volleyer play at the net at all times, except when he is serving or receiving the serve. With his partner at the net, the good groundstroker can remain in the backcourt, using his strong drives to maneuver the opponents into making weak shots. The opposing players, regardless of whether they stay in the backcourt or come to the net, will have to keep their returns away from the net man because any shots he can reach will be volleyed away by him for winners. This one-up, one-back style of play can be very effective when used at the high school level. We saw two boys win a State High School Doubles Championship by using it. It is rarely effective against a team of really good volleyers, however.

In order to be a good doubles player, each member of a team should have definite rules to guide his play. That is how team work is developed. Even though it may look as if members of a smooth-working doubles team are acting together instinctively, such is not usually the case. They may move together and work together smoothly because they have either agreed beforehand or have discovered through previous experience that it is to their advantage to play certain shots in a certain manner and to react in a definite manner to various specific situations. Here are some principles of play which will make you a better doubles player:

When your team is serving: (1) Get the first serve in and to the backhand of your opponent. The best serve in doubles is an American twist serve which bounces high to the backhand of your opponent. The high bounce forces the service returner to hit a high backhand groundstroke, which is one of the most difficult shots in the game. (2) Run in as far as possible to volley the service return, but stop just before your opponent strokes the ball so that you may move again to reach the ball. (3) The first volley is the important one. If your opponents are in the backcourt, hit the ball deep to one of their backhands; if they are in the one-up, one-back formation, volley it at the feet of the man returning the serve.

When your team is receiving the serve: (1) Unless it is a weak serve do not try to win the point outright on your return. Instead, try to hit it low to the feet of the incoming server. (2) Mix in a few lobs with your drives. (3) Play the one-up, one-back formation only if you have good returns of serve. If the opponents' serves are difficult to handle, stay in the backcourt and wait for a later opportunity to go to the net.

During a rally after you have returned the serve and your opponents are at the net: (1) Seldom, if ever, should you attempt to drive the ball past them if you are deep in the backcourt. (2) Use a mixture of lobs and low drives in an attempt to force the net players back or to cause a weak, short volley. (3) After a good lob, drive their smash return. Hit it at their feet and advance to the net together.

During a rally when you and your partner are at the net and your opponents are in the backcourt: (1) Keep your volleys on their backhands. (2) Do not be impatient to win the point. Keep the ball in play until you get a high volley to angle, or a short lob to kill. (3) Play their deep lobs carefully, but try to make a deep return with your smash to their backhands.

If doubles partners understand and apply these general principles and few simple rules, they can surely avoid much of the confusion that occurs among uncoordinated teams. Doubles partners need to adopt a frame of mind that, for the duration of their match, makes them want to cause their partner to look good. That is to say, every shot in doubles must be made with your partner in mind. Try to avoid letting the opponents force him into making difficult shots. If there is any doubt about whether your shot will be a winner or a setup, play it cautiously. Don't put your partner on the spot, or in the hole. Try to make him look good. Do not try to win the points by yourself. The best doubles players are not always the hard, spectacular hitters. Instead, they are often the easy, cagey ones who maneuver the opponents and place their shots so well that any high school player can finish off the rally. In this manner, doubles is a team game, and it is usually the team that works together that wins.

11

Mind Your Tennis Manners

Tennis is a competitive game, one which you usually play to win because it's fun to play hard and to beat someone. Not all tennis matches, however, are dog-eat-dog battles in which the sole object is to win. The majority of tennis matches are friendly get-togethers where the players are just as concerned about having an enjoyable match as they are about winning it.

Because you don't play the game alone, the manner in which you conduct yourself while playing and the manner in which you conform to the customs and manners of the game can do much to affect the amount of fun or enjoyment you, and those with whom you play, derive from the time spent on the tennis court.

Many of the manners and customs of the game are not included in the rules. They have been evolved from the experience of players throughout the game's history and are now taken for granted almost as much as are the official rules. The wise and considerate player learns the correct behavior early in his tennis experience and practices it throughout his career.

YOUR TENNIS UNIFORM

As we have told you in an earlier chapter, white has become the traditional color for tennis clothing. Nothing in the rules prevents you from wearing pink shorts or a plaid shirt on the court. However, such attire will bring frowns of disapproval from the tennis committee chairman and better informed players—if not a request to leave the court and retire to the nearest masquerade ball!

A clean, white T-shirt or polo-shirt, white shorts or trousers, low-cut white sneakers, and clean, white wool socks make up the standard outfit for tennis. Shorts should be of the knee-length or medium-length type and not abbreviated basketball or swimming trunks.

For warm-up or for cooling off after the game, a sweater or jacket is advised. Here again, white is preferred although many ranking players are now appearing in clean, neat, colored sweaters. Don't make yours too loud, however; stick to a white or solid navy, yellow, or tan and you will be met with approval in most places.

COURTESY PAYS

To avoid embarrassment to yourself and to those with whom you play, learn and know the basic rules of the game. They have been summarized for you in an earlier chapter. You don't need to know the technicalities and all the fine points involved in the rules, but do learn the basic ones.

In addition to the specific rules of the game, you should be aware of the following customs:

1. Before you serve be sure the receiver is ready to receive the serve. If you have served and if there is any doubt in your mind as to whether or not the receiver was ready to receive the serve, be quick to offer to serve it over.

After a fault on the first serve, avoid serving the second ball too quickly. Give your opponent time to get set for the second ball or to remove the first ball from the playing court, if necessary.

2. When receiving the serve, don't return a ball that is obviously out. Let the ball go past you back to the fence or hit it easily into the bottom of the net where it will not be a hindrance to safe play.

You, as receiver, are responsible for determining whether a served ball is in or out. If the ball lands close to the line and you are not sure whether or not it was a good serve, offer to play a let. (If you have a referee, it is his responsibility to make the decisions. Play them as he calls them—good calls or bad calls, they generally even up in a match.)

3. During a rally, you are the linesman for all balls that land on your side of the net. Play the good balls, saying nothing. Call the close outs and let the obvious outs go by. Again, if any question arises, play a let.

If the rally is interfered with by a ball rolling on your court while a rally is in progress or by a piece of paper blowing around, offer to play a let.

4. When returning balls to the players on an adjacent court, wait until their rally or point is concluded. Then roll or bounce the balls directly to them when they are looking at you.

If your ball rolls onto an adjoining court, wait until play on that court is completed before asking the players there to return the ball to you.

5. If you are a spectator at a match or waiting on the side lines for a court to become free, don't make a nuisance of yourself. Noise, shouting, and loud conversation are all distracting to players on the court. Quiet, subdued conversation is the rule on the court or the side lines.

12

Your First Tournament

There is a general feeling among beginning tennis players that most tennis tournaments are restricted to skilled and experienced players. They feel that tournaments are contests only for players who are champions of some sort or another, winners of some previous titles, or players of much experience. Beginners don't belong in tournaments is the general feeling. Nothing could be farther from the truth!

There are by far a greater number of tournaments for beginners and players of only mediocre ability than for expert and advanced players. Most tournaments are held merely to provide some fun and friendly competition for average or beginning players. The players in these tournaments are the champions of tomorrow—the future greats of tennis who are gaining experience and know-how by meeting other beginners in friendly competition and having a lot of fun while they do so. Because these players are unknowns, or newcomers, to the tennis field, you don't read a great deal about them or their tournaments in the newspapers. The headlines on our sports pages are grabbed by the winners of the many championship tournaments which are held for competition between expert players, but these tournaments are actually few in number compared with those held for novice or beginning players.

If you really want to get a lot of enjoyment out of tennis, play in as many of these novice tournaments as you can. Not only will you test your game, but also you will get a lot of experience playing against various types of players, which will improve your game. Too many players play against the same opponents time and time again. They get in a rut because, after a few matches, each player knows pretty well what the other player can do, and what he will do with certain shots. They miss much of the actual thrill of competition which comes from playing against an unfamiliar opponent.

When beginners are asked or encouraged to enter a tournament, they usually decline with the same, or a similar, comment. As one boy put it: "Me enter a tournament? Not on your life! I'll be darned if I'll make a fool out of myself by getting clobbered that badly." If you are a beginner, you should enter a beginner's tournament, one in which you will be playing against other unskilled players. If you have any luck at all, you might be drawn against someone you can beat, or at least give a good game. If you draw a better player as your opponent, and if you are beaten, even badly, what have you actually lost? Not a great deal, really, because, as a beginner, you probably weren't expected to win. More important, you have gained some valuable experience in playing to win "when the chips are down." In addition, you have probably made some new friends or buddies among the group of players that you have met at the tournament, and you have probably had a lot of fun.

How do you find out when and where tournaments are being held? The simplest way is to ask your park or playground tennis instructor or your school tennis coach. This information becomes available when clubs or parks hold tournaments, and announcements giving all the information about the tournament are usually sent to other clubs and parks, schools, and YMCA's. Whoever is in charge of tennis receives the announcements and posts them on a bulletin board.

A tournament announcement usually tells when and where the tournament will be held, what divisions will be included (that is, whether it will be a Men's tournament, or Boy's, or Junior's and so on), and what, if any, the entry fee will be. It also tells you where to send the entry blank which is attached to the announcement, and who the tournament chairman will be.

There is usually a deadline for entries in a tournament, and it is indicated on the announcement, also. Entries generally must be received by the tournament chairman at least three of four days before the day the tournament is to begin, so get your entry in early. If you mail it, check with the tournament chairman by phone a few days later to be sure it has been received. It may become mislaid or lost, and a phone call will save you the trouble of going to the place where the tournament is being held, only to find that you are not officially entered.

Quite often an entry fee is asked of each entrant and must be sent with the entry blank. Fees vary, ranging from 50 cents in novice tournaments to 5 dollars in Men's Championship Tournaments. The higher entry fees usually cover the cost of balls, which are furnished for each match, and shower and locker facilities, which are provided as a service to players.

If the entry fee is a small one, players are usually expected to furnish their own balls. Each player is requested to furnish three new balls for each match he plays. In such cases it is customary to use only three balls, with the winning player retaining possession of the new balls, and the loser keeping those used during the match.

On the day before the tournament begins, you should check with the tournament chairman, either by phone or in person, to see what time you play and against whom. Regardless of what time you are scheduled for, *be prompt.* If the tournament is a large one, or if only a few courts are available for play, matches will be scheduled at definite times, and players are expected to be on time for their matches. If you are more than just a few minutes late, the tournament chairman can default you and award the match to your opponent. In this case, your opponent won't be any happier than you because he entered the tournament to play tennis, and not to win by default.

If you know you are going to be late for your match, a phone call to the chairman might result in having your match postponed, or delayed, to a time more suitable for you. Don't be angry if you are defaulted, however. Running a tournament is a difficult job, and it is not often easy for a chairman to reschedule a match.

When you report to the courts, check in immediately with the tournament chairman. Let him know you are there, ready to play, and ask him if your opponent is ready. If he tells you that the court to which you are assigned is not yet available, don't wander away from the area. He'll want to get your match started as soon as your court is available, so it's your responsibility to remain in the immediate area. To wander off someplace where you can't be reached will delay things, and you might be defaulted.

If you do have to wait for a court, mingle with the other players who are also waiting. You and they have much in common, being tennis players, and you'll have much to talk about. Compare rackets, talk about your club or park courts, or some interesting tennis player you know. If you talk tennis, they'll listen, and when they talk tennis, you'll probably want to listen, too. You'll make many new, interesting friends this way, and you might even wind up with an invitation to a friendly game at that swanky club on the other side of town.

When you meet your opponent for the first time, shake hands with him as you would when meeting anyone else. He's your opponent, it is true, but you and he can still be friends and have loads of fun during your match. Don't be frightened of him because he's probably just as "green" as you are. If you are playing in a novice tournament, he probably thinks you're as "hot" as you think he is.

As you walk on the court, take charge of things. Measure the net—one racket length and one racket width at the middle, remember (Fig. 37). Spin your racket and ask him to call "rough" or "smooth." Give him the impression that you know what you're doing, and that this tournament business is actually old stuff for you (it isn't really, and you're scared stiff, but don't let him know that!).

Be courteous and polite during the warm-up. Give him whatever practice he wants and ask him to give you the shots you want to practice. When you are ready to go, say, "I'm ready if you are."

Fig. 37. Measuring the net.

Continue to be polite during the match. Be a good sport. Compliment him on his good shots, apologize for any lucky breaks you get, and say a few pleasant words to him as you pass each other when changing sides. Play the game fairly, giving him the benefit of any doubtful calls that come up.

If your opponent is surly and sarcastic, or if he is a poor sport, about the only alternative is to enjoy the game as best you can and avoid him in the future. Don't get down to his level by being sarcastic, too; you'll gain nothing from it.

Regardless of the outcome of the match, or the manner in which your opponent conducted himself on the court, shake hands with him after the final point. If you lost, thank him for the game and tell him how much you enjoyed it. If you won, comment about having played over your head, or about the bad luck he had. If you both had fun, and if you think he'd enjoy it, ask him to play a friendly game with you some time on your home courts.

When your match is completed, try to stay around the courts and watch some of the other players. You can learn a lot about their games which can help you if you have to play them later, or in some other tournament. Mingle with the others again, too, making as many friends as you can. Judging by what we've seen happen at Junior tournaments, you'll soon have enough tennis buddies with whom you can make more tennis dates than you have time for.

TYPES OF TOURNAMENTS

There are several different types of tennis tournaments which are conducted by tennis clubs, parks, and playgrounds. The most popular type of tournament is called a Single Elimination Tournament. In this type, the names of the players entered in the tournament are placed in a container, "drawn" blindly, and then listed in the order they were drawn. The first two players on the list play against each other, the next two players play against each other, and so on, until all players have played a match. Losers of each match are eliminated from the tournament, while winners advance, moving from the first round (their first match) to the second round; if they then win, they go to the third round. When only eight players are left in the tournament, they will be in the quarter-final round; when only four players are left, they will be in the semi-final round; and when only two players are left, they will be in the finals. The winner of the final round is the champion, and the loser is the runner-up.

If the total number of players entered in the tournament does not equal 8, 16, 32, or 64, it will be necessary to assign "byes" to certain players in the first round. A "bye" means merely that the player who has drawn it automatically advances into the second round, where there will then be an even number of players, either 4, 8, 16, 32, or 64. "Byes" are assigned to specific places in the draw according to the regulations of the United States Lawn Tennis Association.

In order to prevent the best players from meeting each other during the early rounds of a tournament, it is common practice to place, or "seed," them in the draw. Seeding is usually determined by record, reputation, or ranking. The list of seeded players, in order of their rank, is posted before the draw is made. As their names are drawn, they are also placed in specific places in the draw sheet, in accordance with USLTA regulations. The No. 1 and No. 2 seeded players are placed so that they will not meet each other until the final round—assuming, of course, that neither of them loses before reaching the finals.

Quite frequently, in order to give the losers of the first round matches more play, clubs will hold Double Elimination Tournaments or Consolation Tournaments. In a Double Elimination Tournament, a player must lose twice before he is eliminated from the tournament; in a Consolation Tournament the losers of first round matches compete with each other for a consolation championship, while the winners of the first round matches compete for the regular championship. The rules regarding the draw for these tournaments are similar to those for the Single Elimination Tournament.

Many tennis clubs maintain a "challenge ladder" throughout the tennis season to provide continuous competition for club members. A ladder is started by listing the names of players vertically on a board in accordance with ability, with the best player on top of the ladder, and the poorest player on the bottom. A player can challenge a man two or three places above to a match. If the challenger wins the match, he changes places on the challenge board with the loser. If the challenged player wins, he is allowed to challenge a player who is listed above him before he must accept another challenge. Rules for ladder tournaments vary somewhat, and are usually posted beside the ladder itself.

13

More About Tournaments and Rankings

Whether you are an expert tennis player, a beginner, an enthusiastic spectator of the game, or a casual reader of the sports page in your local newspaper, you should know a little about who governs and controls tennis play in our country in order better to understand and appreciate the game.

The organization that controls the game in the United States is the United States Lawn Tennis Association, generally referred to as the USLTA. Its chief function is to supervise play of the game and to interpret and enforce the rules and regulations of tennis as adopted by the organization that supervises play of the game throughout the world—the International Tennis Federation.

There are a number of regional and sectional tennis associations throughout our country, each of which is a member of the USLTA. The country is divided, geographically, into a number of different areas. Many of these areas have tennis associations that are members of the USLTA. For example, the following associations are members: The California Lawn Tennis Association, the Eastern Lawn Tennis Association, the Western Lawn Tennis Association, the Missouri Valley Lawn Tennis Association, and the New England Lawn Tennis Association. The officers of these, and many other regional and sectional associations, attend annual meetings of the USLTA and elect officers and committee members who then conduct the affairs of the USLTA for the coming year.

In addition to supervising play of the game in the United States and enforcing and interpreting the rules and regulations of the game, the USLTA also conducts tournaments either by itself or through its member associations. All "official" tennis tournaments are sanctioned by the United States Lawn Tennis Association. The United States Lawn Tennis Association official age groups for tournaments are given in the following list.

1. Boy's Singles and Doubles (for boys 15 years of age and under)
2. Junior Singles and Doubles (for boys 16 to 18 years of age)
3. Men's Singles and Doubles (for men over 18)
4. Men's Senior Singles and Doubles (for men over 45)

There are similar age divisions for girls and women. You, as a younger player, will be playing in either the boy's or the junior division, although you are also eligible to play in the men's division.

At the close of the tennis year, sometime in early winter, a Ranking Committee of the USLTA meets and publishes a ranking of tennis players of the country for the divisions we mentioned. These rankings are based on the Ranking Committee's judgment of the players' performance in sanctioned tournaments and matches for the previous tennis year. The important tournaments, as far as rankings go, for boys and juniors are the *Western* and *National* Boy's and Junior Championship. Rankings for the men's division are determined principally by a player's performance in a series of week-long grass court tournaments that are usually held on the East Coast during the summer. This series of tournaments, sometimes referred to as the "tennis circuit," generally is held at private clubs in the East. These tournaments are usually open only to players of proven ability or with high national or sectional rankings.

One of the major activities of the USLTA is its Junior Development Program. Through its fifteen sectional tennis associations and their Tennis Patrons Associations, the USLTA is stimulating interest through colleges, clubs, playground and recreation departments in cities and towns in the nation by conducting tennis classes and clinics, team matches, tournaments, and exhibitions. Almost all the ranking senior players have gained experience by playing through first the boy's and then the junior divisions and are a product of the USLTA's Junior Development Program. When a youngster shows promise, the USLTA is quick to encourage the development of his game. He is often given special coaching and is invited to play in special tournaments to gain further playing experience.

Tennis in the high schools

In recent years, tennis has become an increasingly important part of the collegiate and high school sports programs. Your high school undoubtedly has a tennis team that competes with other high schools in the city and state to decide city and state champions. When two high school tennis teams meet each other, the winner of a match can be decided in several different ways. The method favored by most schools is this: The schools play each other five singles and four doubles matches, and the team that wins five or more of these matches wins the particular team match. Quite often players are permitted to play in only one event in these matches—either singles or doubles.

In addition to matches between schools, state high school tennis associations also conduct state championship tournaments. Players qualify for the state finals by competing in a series of sectional or district elimination tournaments. Players who win these tournaments then get together to compete with each other in the finals for the state championship. Points are scored for the team or school which the player represents when that player wins a match. At the conclusion of the tournament, points are totaled and the team or school champion is decided. Individual champions, of course, are also determined.

14

A Practice Schedule for Beginning Players

First and second days on the court

Your first and second periods on the court should be confined to work on the Forehand Groundstroke only, with steady practice of the swing, hitting a dropped ball, and hitting a tossed ball.

1. Take turns practicing the swing and coaching each other (15-20 minutes).
2. Take turns hitting a dropped ball and coaching each other (20-30 minutes).
3. Close the periods by hitting a tossed ball and coaching each other (20-30 minutes).

You have now worked on the first three stages of the forehand groundstroke. As you know, we have suggested tests for you to take, at each stage, which will show you how well you are progressing. You probably won't be able to pass these tests during the first few days on the court, but you will undoubtedly make some progress at each stage. If you follow our plan, you will gradually pass each test and move along from stage to stage.

Third day on the court

1. Spend the first part of the period reviewing the forehand swing, hitting a dropped ball, and hitting a tossed ball on the forehand. Try to pass the test for each of these stages (15-20 minutes).
2. Start work on running to hit a tossed ball (20 minutes).
3. Start work on the backhand swing (15 minutes).
4. Practice hitting a tossed ball on the backhand (20 minutes).
5. Start on the serve, hitting the ball against a fence.
6. Rally (15-20 minutes). To start a rally, one player drops and hits to his Buddy, who then tries to return the ball. Both players then

try to keep the ball in play, playing it on the first bounce and at waist level, or nearly so.

Fourth day on the court

1. Review previous stages for the forehand and try to pass the tests (15-20 minutes).
2. Review backhand swing and hitting a tossed ball with the backhand (20 minutes).
3. Work on running to hit a tossed ball on the backhand (20 minutes).
4. Practice the serve against a fence (15 minutes).
5. Practice the serve on the court. One player can serve over and over again, and his Buddy can practice returning the serve (15–20 minutes).
6. Rally (20 minutes).

Fifth day on the court

1. Review previous stages for the forehand and backhand strokes. Try to pass the tests for various stages (30-40 minutes).
2. Rally (20 minutes).
3. Practice serves, on the court, one player serving and the other returning the serve (15 minutes).
4. Play a few games according to the rules of tennis. (Refer to rules and scoring section of book.) When playing, we suggest that the server be given three serves for each point. In regular tennis, of course, the server is given only two serves for each point; if he serves a double fault, he loses the point. For practice purposes, however, we found it helpful for the server to be given three serves.

   If you can't hold three balls in your left hand while serving, hold two and put the third in your pocket or lay it at your feet; in any case, have three balls ready each time you start a point.

   When serving here, hit the first two serves overhand, using the regular service swing. If neither of the first two serves is good, use the drop-and-hit (the feeder stroke) for a third serve, merely trying to get the ball in play to start a rally.

Sixth day on the court

After about five periods on the court, you will probably have passed the tests for the dropped ball and the tossed ball for the forehand stroke.

1. Review the previous stages. Try to pass tests you have not already passed (20 minutes).

2. Practice serve on the court (20 minutes).
3. Rally (20 minutes).
4. Play one set.

Seventh day on the court

1. Review previous stages for the forehand and backhand.
2. Practice serves and returns of serves.
3. Start work on the volley, forehand, and backhand.
4. Start work on the overhead smash.
5. Rally.
6. Play.

You will notice from the above outline that we suggest that you begin rallying and serving during the third period on the court. You won't be able to do these things well, that is, you won't be able to rally well, nor will you be able to serve well, but you will be practicing them. We have found that starting these particular activities early in your career, together with the forehand and backhand strokes, leads to the development of a well-rounded type of game with no particular or no undue emphasis on any one stroke. You will be working on the forehand, backhand, and the serve each time you walk on the court after the third lesson. It has been our experience that this is the best procedure in developing a well-rounded game. Many players tend to spend too much time on the development of one particular stroke (the forehand, for example) and learn this stroke to the exclusion of others. The well-rounded tennis player, of course, has a good forehand, a good backhand, and a good serve. To learn each of these strokes well it is important that you spend considerable time on each of them and not work on only one stroke to the exclusion of the others.

After six or seven practice periods, both you and your Buddy should be quite adept at dropping and hitting the ball directly to your point-of-aim. From this point on, then, we suggest that you follow the method that tennis professionals use in working with pupils. One of you can assume the role of the professional and attempt only to feed the other player whatever shots he needs practice on. For example, if your Buddy is weak on the backhand stroke, you assume the role of the professional. In this capacity, you merely drop and hit the balls to his backhand time and time again, setting them up for him in such a manner that he can get the practice that he needs. If it is forehand practice that he needs, of course, you can hit to his forehand. The thing to keep in mind, however, is that you are *helping* him by feeding him the shots that he needs practice on.

Each time you and your Buddy step on the tennis court, you should have something in mind that you or he or both of you are going to practice. In other words, you should have in mind some specific stroke that you are going to be working on. One of you should assume the feeder role, or the role of the professional, and give practice to the person who needs it by feeding him these balls.

PRACTICE DRILL SCORE CHART

	FOREHANDS								BACKHANDS						SERVES			
DATE	DROP-AND-HIT		HIT TOSSED BALL		RUN AND HIT TOSSED BALL		RALLY RECORD		HIT TOSSED BALL		RUN AND HIT TOSSED BALL		RALLY RECORD		FROM RIGHT COURT		FROM LEFT COURT	
	A	B	A	B	A	B	A	B	A	B	A	B	A	B	A	B	A	B

INSTRUCTIONS:

1. Player A uses column A; Player B uses column B.
2. For forehands and backhands, record number of consecutive good shots.
3. For serves, record number of good shots out of 50 tries.

PLAYERS:

A. ______________________

B. ______________________

Glossary

ACE. An earned point, usually made by serving. Applies generally to a winning shot which one's opponent fails to touch with his racket.

ADVANTAGE. The point scored after deuce.

ALLEY. Part of the tennis court lying between the singles and doubles side lines.

AMERICAN TWIST. Type of serve in which racket strikes the ball with an upward motion, causing the ball to spin during flight and to take a high bounce.

BACKHAND. Stroke used to hit a ball that comes to a player on his left side (right-handed player).

BACKSPIN. Backward spin on the ball, with ball revolving in reverse direction from its flight.

BASE LINE GAME. A style of play. Player stays on or near his base line and seldom moves into the fore court.

CHANGE OF PACE. Changing, or mixing up, the speed of your shots.

CHOP. A downward stroke at the ball, imparting backspin to it.

CROSS COURT SHOT. A ball hit diagonally across the court, from one corner to the diagonally opposite corner.

DAVIS CUP. Cup for which nations of the world compete with each other. Winning of it is symbolic of world supremacy in amateur tennis.

"DINK." To hit the ball easily and high so that it lands deep in the court. A steady, consistent, low-speed type of play.

DOUBLE FAULT. Two successive faults in serving.

DOUBLES. A match in which two teams of two players each oppose each other.

DOWN-THE-LINE SHOT. A ball driven parallel to a side line.

DRIVE. Full swing stroke used to hit a ball after it bounces (groundstroke).

DRIVE VOLLEY. Full swing stroke used to hit a ball before it bounces ("on-the-fly").

DROP SHOT. Chopping the ball, imparting backspin to it, and hitting it so that it barely clears the net and lands only a few feet from it.

FAULT. A serve that does not land in the proper service court.

FOOT FAULT. A violation of the service rule, usually stepping on or over the base line, or jumping off the ground when serving.

FOREHAND. Stroke used to hit a ball that comes to a player on his right side (right-handed player).

FORWARD SPIN. Forward revolving motion of the ball, with ball revolving in the direction of its flight (same as top spin).

GROUNDSTROKE. Stroke used to hit a ball after it has bounced.

HALF-VOLLEY. A "pick-up" stroke used to hit the ball immediately after it strikes the ground.

"HIT-THROUGH-THE-BALL." Moving the racket head along the intended line of flight of the ball, as contrasted with moving the racket head across the intended line of flight.

Hold service. Winning the game that you are serving.

Let. Any point that has to be replayed.

Lob. A high, arching shot that is hit over a net man's head and deep into his backcourt.

Love. A scoring term, indicating "nothing," or "zero."

Love game. A game in which the loser has not won a point.

Love set. A set in which the loser has not won a game.

Match point. Final point needed to win a match.

Mixed doubles. A match in which two teams, consisting of a boy and a girl each, oppose each other.

Net game. Manner in which a player plays in the forecourt, close to the net, and volleys.

Passing shot. Shot hit past a man at the net so that he can't reach the ball.

Poaching. Generally applied to play at the net in doubles or mixed doubles when one player plays a ball that should have been played by his partner.

Rally. A prolonged series of strokes, groundstrokes, and/or volleys.

Serve. The act of putting the ball into play at the start of a point by throwing it into the air and hitting it.

Service break. Winning your opponent's serve: "breaking through" to win the game your opponent is serving.

Singles. A match in which one player opposes another player.

Top spin. Same as forward spin. Forward revolving motion of the ball.

USLTA. United States Lawn Tennis Association, the governing body of the game in the United States.

Volley. A stroke made by hitting the ball "on-the-fly," before it has touched the ground.

Index